GREAT SEA DISASTERS

THE WORLD'S WORST SEA DISASTERS

GREAT SEA DISASTERS

THE WORLD'S WORST SEA DISASTERS

NEIL WILSON

This is a Siena book

Siena is an imprint of Parragon

First published in Great Britain in 1998 by
Parragon
13 Whiteladies Road, Clifton
Bristol BS8 1PB

ISBN: 0-75252-743-6

Printed in Italy

Edited, designed and produced by Haldane Mason, London

Acknowledgements
Art Director: Ron Samuels
Editorial Director: Sydney Francis
Managing Editor: Charles Dixon-Spain
Editor: Ian Penburthy
Design: Caroline Grimshaw
Picture Research: Charles Dixon-Spain and Elizabeth Towers

Picture Acknowledgements:

Associated Press; 74: Barnaby's Picture Library; 13, 15 (Vic Earp), 20 (Robin Dawson), 23, 69, 77 (© Dorien Leigh Ltd. (Chace)), 78
(Top), 79, 82 (Andrew Besley): E. T. Archive; 11, 18, 39, 42: Hulton Picture Library; 1, 2, 7 (Both), 10, 14, 26, 35, 36, 40, 43, 44,
47, 55, 56, 66, 70, 72, 83, 84, 91, 92, 93: Kobal Collection; Front cover (courtesy of 20th-Century Fox): Mary Evans Picture
Library; Back cover right, 16, 17, 22, 41, 45 (Right), 50, 51, 58 (*from* Cassell's 'Illustrated History of England'), 59, 76, 78 (Bottom),
80, 81, 90: National Maritime Museum; 30, 45 (Left), 49, 53, 54, 88: Rex Features; Back cover top left, 9 (Tom Kidd), 61 (Leon
Schadeberg) 63, 65, 73, 94, 95: Topham Picture Point; 28, 52, 62, 64, 75: World's Edge Picture Library; Back cover bottom left, 6,
8, (Both), 21, 24, 32, 48, 68, 86

Half-title page: *An artist's impression on
the White Star Liner* Atlantic *aground on
Meagher Island, Nova Scotia, in 1873. 560
lives were lost in the disaster.*

Page 2: *Impending disaster. Ernest
Shackleton's ship, the* Endurance, *trapped in
the pack ice of the Weddell Sea in 1915.*

CONTENTS

THOSE IN PERIL ON THE SEA

The seafarer's trade has always been fraught with danger. It has been estimated that the remains of some 250,000 vessels, ranging in age from mediaeval to modern, and in size from fishing smack to supertanker, lie scattered on the sea-bed around the shores of the British Isles alone. The equivalent figure for all the world's oceans defies comprehension.

Above: *Grace Darling, daughter of the Farne Islands lighthouse keeper, became a national heroine after the wreck of the* Forfarshire *in 1838.*

Left: *Early seafarers were exposed to many dangers, not least of which was making landfall on an uncharted shore. This dramatic painting shows a Dutch vessel in distress.*

Below: *The magnetic compass was a delicate instrument, and as navigation became more precise many methods were developed for protecting and adjusting it.*

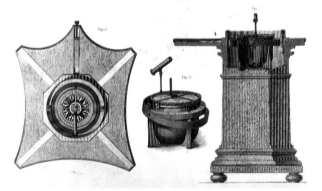

COMPASS CORRECTOR AND SPRING SUSPENSION COMPASS.

Our long relationship with the sea has always been one of balancing risk against reward. Once, ships were – and to a certain extent still are – the only economical means of transporting large quantities of cargo and, until the advent of commercial airlines, they offered the only form of intercontinental travel. For many centuries, huge profits have been made by those who invested in ships and shipping, but the associated risks – the 'Adventures and Perils' referred to in the classic Lloyd's Marine Insurance Policy of 1779 – were also considerable. However, when disaster occurred, the owners of the ship and her cargo could always make a claim on their insurers, a fact that would have provided little consolation for the sailors and passengers as they fought for their lives aboard the sinking vessel.

The most common causes of disaster at sea are stranding, collision, foundering and fire, although the reasons for each can range from sheer bad luck to criminal negligence. However, there is almost always an element of human error involved, and from the earliest days of sail to the current era of supertankers and satellites, seafarers have sought ways of making their perilous profession a little safer. Some of their most important achievements in this respect are outlined in this chapter; the remainder of this book examines some of the worst disasters in the history of man's long contest with the sea.

CHART AND COMPASS

One of the seafarer's fundamental needs is to know where he is and where he is bound, and how to avoid danger in the form of rocks, reefs and shallow waters. In ancient times, most sea voyages would have been made by following the coast, never venturing out of sight of land for very long, and navigating by reference to visible landmarks. This technique, known as pilotage, was used by the crews of Arab dhows to trade regularly with India in the first century BC, and may have allowed Phoenician sailors to circumnavigate the African continent 500 years earlier. But successful longer voyages, sailing out of sight of land for long periods, required a knowledge of scientific navigation, which began to develop seriously after the discovery of the New World in the 15th century.

As explorers ventured across the world's oceans, they collected navigational information in their logs and plotted it on their charts. The idea of defining positions on the earth's surface using imaginary lines of latitude and longitude had originated with the ancient Greek astronomer

The most common causes of disaster at sea are stranding, collision, foundering and fire, although the reasons for each can range from sheer bad luck to criminal negligence.

Above: *Navigational charts were once precious documents, containing vital information gathered over many decades. This French chart of the Indian Ocean dates from the 17th century.*

Hipparchus of Rhodes, in the second century BC, and was transmitted to western Europe through the works of Arabic scholars. Even in Hipparchus' day, latitude could be measured to within a quarter of a degree, but it was not until the 18th century that longitude could be determined at sea with a similar level of accuracy.

It must have taken courage and audacity to sail into uncharted waters, and even those who followed in the wake of the pioneers faced great danger and uncertainty. The instructions given to the master of the *Batavia*, for example (see pages 19–20), on her voyage from the Cape of Good Hope to Java, were simply: 'Sail on latitude south 36 to 42 degrees for 2,400 to 3,000 miles [3,860 to 4,830 kilometres], then steer north to the Sunda Strait'. It is little wonder that many early expeditions met with complete disaster.

Finding latitude by measuring the altitude of the Pole Star or the sun was a relatively straight-forward task that had been mastered by the time of Columbus, but a reliable method for determining longitude at sea had to wait for the development of the marine chronometer in the late 18th century. This meant that long voyages to east or west were potentially dangerous because, without accurate knowledge of the longitude, it was difficult to know when to expect a landfall.

Astro-navigation depended on clear skies. When sun and stars were hidden by clouds, the mariner navigated by 'dead-reckoning' (DR), extrapolating from his last accurate position using the ship's speed and compass heading. While this was fine for short periods, more than a few days of DR could lead to serious navigational errors as the ship was deflected from her estimated course by winds and

Right: *The first steam-powered vessels appeared at the beginning of the 19th century, but most steamships continued to carry the insurance of a sailing rig until the early 1900s.*

NAVIGATION

In clear weather, the old sailors would steer by the sun and the stars, but to hold an accurate course in overcast conditions and over long distances required another means of determining direction.

Left: *The oil tanker* Braer *suffered engine failure during a storm and was driven ashore in Shetland in 1996. No lives were lost but her leaking cargo caused widespread pollution.*

currents – as happened with the *Neva* (see page 25) and the liner *Atlantic* (see pages 37–9). The combination of astro-navigation and DR continued to be relied on by ocean-crossing vessels until the advent of satellite navigation systems, which have become prevalent in the last 30 years.

The lack of accurate charts was another factor that led to many wrecks and strandings, as evinced by the 'uncharted rock' that sank the *Birkenhead* (see pages 49–50). In 18th-century Britain, naval officers still had to find (and pay for) their own charts and pilot books, and in the wars with France more ships were lost because of poor navigational information than through enemy action. It was not until 1795 that George III set up the Admiralty Hydrographic Office to produce accurate charts of the world's oceans, and throughout the 19th

century, ships of the Royal Navy laboriously sounded the sea-bed using hand-leads and sounding machines. In clear weather, the old sailors would steer by the sun and the stars, but to hold an accurate course in overcast conditions and over long distances required another means of determining direction. The magnetic compass was probably invented independently by both Chinese and Italian navigators, the earliest written European references dating from the early 12th century. By 1380, the card compass had been invented. This comprised a magnetized needle attached to a pivoted card marked with 'points' from which bearings could be read. Later, a 'lubber line' was added to the compass bowl; this was lined up fore-and-aft, so that the ship's heading could be read directly from the compass.

STEAM POWER

The advent of steam power in the early 19th century promised to free seafarers from the constraints of wind and tide, but it would be many years before engines were powerful enough.

However, a magnetic compass needle does not point to the geographical North Pole, but to the magnetic pole, a point that gradually changes position from year to year (at present, it is located in northern Canada). The angle between True North and Magnetic North is called variation, which also changes with time and with position. It took several centuries for the effects of variation to be understood and allowed for. In the meantime, many ships were lost (see *Association*, page 20). The early 20th century saw the development of the gyrocompass, which has no magnetic sensor, but relies instead on the force of gravity, the rotation of the earth and the properties of the gyroscope to point to True North.

STEAM, IRON AND STEEL

The main driving force behind major advances in ship design has almost always been commercial interest. The need for the economical transport of cargo and passengers over longer distances led to the building of ever bigger, faster and more efficient ships. A second impetus was the desire for military advantage, which led to the development of bigger and more heavily armed battleships, and to completely new kinds of vessel, like the submarine and the aircraft carrier.

But many accidents have occurred during periods of innovation. New and untested designs often exhibited unforeseen stability problems or structural defects that did not become apparent until disaster struck, as in the foundering of top-heavy wooden warships in the 16th and 17th centuries (see *Mary Rose*, page 17–19, and *Vasa*, page 20) and the iron-clad battleships of the late 19th century (see *Captain*, pages 50–51). Moreover, such hazards are not confined to the past – in recent years, it has been argued that 'ro-ro' ferries (see page 62) and large bulk carriers, like the *Derbyshire* (see page 89), suffer from dangerous flaws in their design.

The advent of steam power in the early 19th century promised to free seafarers from the constraints of wind and tide, but it would be many decades before engines were powerful enough to drive a ship against heavy weather or hold her safely off a lee shore. In the meantime, the 'iron

Right: *At the time of her launching in 1858, I. K. Brunel's* Great Eastern *was the largest ship in the world. She was revolutionary in design, and formed the prototype of the modern ocean liner.*

topsail' introduced the added dangers of fire and explosion (see *Sultana*, page 57). Steam power was mistrusted at first, and most steamships continued to carry sails until the end of the 19th century.

In parallel with the introduction of the steam engine came the use of iron (and later steel) as a shipbuilding material, which allowed the construction of bigger and stronger hulls. The supreme example of the iron ship was Brunel's *Great Eastern*, launched in 1858, which was the forerunner of the huge, screw-driven steamships that would replace the smaller and less seaworthy paddle steamers over the next few decades.

The first scheduled steamship services across the Atlantic began in 1838, and it was competition for this route that provided the main impetus for advances in the speed, size and comfort of ocean liners over the next 100 years. In the 1850s, the average transatlantic steamer was 200–300 feet (61–91 metres) long and paddle-driven. Such ships took 10–14 days to cross; in the 1870s, length had increased to 300–400 feet (91–122 metres) and speed to 16 knots (30 kph), reducing the crossing time to seven or eight days; by the time the *Titanic*

was built in 1912, screw-driven liners had grown to 900 feet (274 metres) and achieved average speeds of 22–27 knots (41–50 kph), crossing the Atlantic in only four or five days.

But the great advances of the late 19th and early 20th centuries led to a dangerous situation, for it was believed that marine engineers had finally succeeded in designing the unsinkable ship. The loss of the *Titanic* (see page 39–43), undoubtedly the most famous sea disaster of all time, was a prime example of technology encouraging such a feeling of invincibility that normal seamanlike practice was put aside.

Although he had been warned by other ships that there were icebergs in the vicinity, the master of the *Titanic* took a calculated risk. It was the liner's maiden voyage and his last before retirement, and no doubt he was keen to make an impressively fast crossing. That there were not enough lifeboats merely compounded the tragedy – the collision should never have happened in the first place. A prudent skipper would not have recklessly endangered his ship by steaming at full speed on a moonless night into an area of known danger.

RADIO AND RADAR

One of the biggest contributions to safety at sea was the development of radio communications in the first half of the 20th century. Marconi made the first transatlantic radio transmission from Mullion Cove in Cornwall in 1901, and two years later the Cunard steamer *Lucania* became the first ship to carry wireless equipment that allowed her to communicate with both sides of the Atlantic. At first, the wireless was used mainly by passengers to send telegrams to relatives and business associates during their voyages – the *Titanic*'s radio operator was so busy sending passengers' greetings in the hours preceding the disaster that when the *Californian* tried to send an ice warning, he brusquely told her to shut up and get off the air.

But the true value of radio was that it allowed ships to warn each other of dangers such as bad weather and ice, to call for assistance when they were in distress, and to inform other vessels of their positions. It was the inquiry into the *Titanic* disaster that first recommended that ships be required to maintain a 24-hour listening watch on the radio – when the *Titanic* went down, the liner *Californian* was only about 12 miles (19 kilometres) distant, but her radio room had closed down for the night and did not receive the fatal SOS message.

Another way in which radio should have contributed to marine safety was by allowing ships in potential collision situations to communicate with each other and clarify their intentions. But there were difficulties (if the master couldn't see the other ship's name, how could he call her on the radio?), and in practice many ships did not use their equipment in this way. The court of inquiry into the collision between the North Sea ferries *European Gateway* and *Speedlink Vanguard*, off Harwich in 1980, found that, if the captains of the two ships had been in direct communication by VHF radio, the disaster would have been avoided.

Radar (short for 'radio detection and ranging') was developed in the 1930s as a means of detecting enemy aircraft, although the principle had been demonstrated by the German scientist Christian Hülsmeyer as early as 1904. The French liner *Normandie* was fitted with a primitive UHF 'iceberg

detector' in 1935, but it was not until after World War 2 that marine radar came into widespread use on merchant vessels. Today, every vessel of more than 500 grt (1,400 cubic metres) (see 'Measurement of Tonnage', page 15) is legally required to carry radar, and vessels over 10,000 grt (28,000 cubic metres) must carry at least two radars.

But for radar equipment to contribute effectively to a ship's safety in conditions of poor visibility, it must be in working order, be switched on, and used correctly by a trained officer who regularly plots the positions of other vessels – requirements that often were not met in the decades following its introduction. As recently as 1980, navigation expert A.N. Cockcroft could write: 'Radar provided a means of detecting other vessels at increased range in restricted visibility and of determining their movements and the risk of collision, but these advantages were negated by the improper use of the equipment and the tendency of radar-equipped ships to maintain full speed. Investigations of collisions involving vessels using radar in restricted visibility almost invariably reveal that adequate plotting has not been carried out.' In the collisions that sank the *Andrea Doria* (see page 46–7) and the *Atlantic Empress* (see page 73–4), all the vessels involved were equipped with radar.

These problems have been tackled in recent years through improved training for watch officers and the introduction of radar surveillance and VTS (Vessel Traffic Services – the marine equivalent of Air Traffic Control) in congested sea areas such as the Dover Strait.

RULES AND REGULATIONS

The International Regulations for Preventing Collisions at Sea are based on British rules formulated in 1862, and became accepted around the world following a conference in Washington in 1889. The 'Rules of the Road at Sea', as they are known, dictate in detail the actions that ships must take in the presence of other vessels, and specify the lights and signals that they must display. Infringement of the rules is accepted in courts of law as evidence of liability.

JUDGEMENT

The court of inquiry into the collision between two North Sea ferries, off Harwich in 1980, found that if the captains had been in direct communication by VHF radio, the disaster would have been avoided.

THE MEASUREMENT OF TONNAGE

Deadweight tonnage (dwt)
The maximum carrying capacity of a cargo ship or oiltanker, including cargo, fuel, crew and stores, expressed in long tons (1 long ton = 2,240 pounds = 1.016 tonnes).

Displacement tonnage
The weight of water displaced by a ship in normal sea-going condition (and, therefore, equal to the actual weight of the ship and everything in her), expressed in long tons or tonnes; used in defining the size of naval vessels (also used by US merchant ships).

Gross registered tonnage (grt)
The total enclosed volume of a merchant ship, expressed in volumetric tons (1 volumetric ton = 100 cubic feet = 2.8 cubic metres); the figure entered on a ship's registration papers and used for assessing harbour dues, canal fees, etc.

Net registered tonnage (nrt)
The volume of space available for carrying cargo and/or paying passengers; equal to the grt less deductions for crew accommodation, engine rooms, fuel bunkers, ballast space, etc.

Left: The sea has always been a dangerous place and the lives of many sailors and fishermen continue to be lost each year.

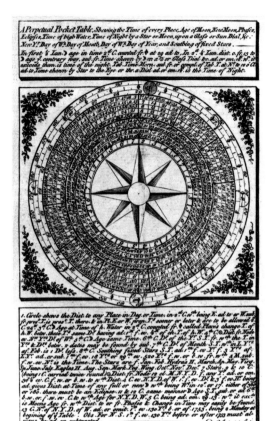

Above: A perpetual pocket table. Tables like these were used by 17th-century seamen.

The International Maritime Organization (IMO) was established by the United Nations in 1958 with the objective of improving safety at sea. It has over 150 member states and promotes the adoption of international conventions and codes concerning maritime safety, the prevention of marine pollution and related matters. Among its important achievements have been the following international conventions: the Safety of Life at Sea (SOLAS); the Prevention of Pollution from Ships; and the Standards of Training, Certification and Watch-keeping for Seafarers. However, it is not the role of the IMO to enforce these regulations; that job lies with the governments of the nations that ratify the conventions, and there is often a lengthy period of debate and procrastination between the adoption of a convention and its coming into force. The SOLAS Convention of 1974, for example, did not come into force until 1980. Since 1980, more than a dozen amendments have been added to SOLAS in the light of subsequent disasters.

SATELLITES AND RESCUE SERVICES

Seafaring has changed more in the last three decades than in the previous 3,000 years, the principal reason being the development of microprocessors and satellite systems for communications, weather tracking and position fixing. Sputnik 1, the first man-made satellite, went into orbit on 4 October 1957, and by 1964 the US Navy had developed the Transit satellite navigation system for fixing the position of its nuclear submarines. Thirty years later, it is possible to buy, for less than £200, a global positioning system (GPS) receiver barely larger than a mobile phone that will give your position anywhere on the planet to within 165 feet (50 metres).

The benefits of another recent high-tech initiative, the Global Maritime Distress and Safety System (GMDSS), were dramatically demonstrated by the rescue of the yachtsmen Tony Bullimore and Thierry Dubois from the Southern Ocean in 1997 (see page 94–5). GMDSS is a world-wide network of satellite and radio communications systems that automatically alerts rescue authorities and transmits the position of a vessel in distress when a radio operator doesn't have time to send an SOS or mayday call. This is achieved by means of an emergency position-indicating radio-beacon (EPIRB), which is carried on the ship and is activated automatically by immersion in sea water. It then sends out a distress signal and position, which are relayed by satellite to a maritime rescue co-ordination centre. Another feature of GMDSS is the Navtex system. This receives and prints out broadcasts of maritime safety information, such as severe weather warnings, which could prevent an accident from happening in the first place. In 1988, the IMO amended SOLAS to require ships to fit GMDSS equipment.

THE HUMAN FACTOR

Despite all the technological advances of the last 100 years, the oldest, and still the most important, safeguard against disaster at sea is the judgement and experience of the ship's master, and the competence of her crew. The captain's knowledge of how his ship will handle in various conditions, his skills in navigation and pilotage, his assessment of weather and sea conditions, and his prudence in situations when danger threatens – all contribute to the safety of his vessel. In recent years, these age-old attributes have had the assistance of high technology in the form of radio communications, gyrocompasses, radar and satellite navigation. But while such advances have undoubtedly made the sailor's lot safer, on occasion they have also lulled him into a false sense of security and dulled the old sea-dog's cautious instincts.

The records of disaster at sea through the centuries tell a remarkable tale of widespread indifference to safety, especially among those who own and operate shipping companies. It is only recently, in the latter part of the 20th century, that concerted international efforts have been made to draw up and enforce safety regulations governing the design, construction and navigation of ships. But even today, despite the best efforts of the IMO and the national marine safety agencies, large numbers of vessels continue to be lost each year. At the end of the day, we find that we cannot legislate against human error.

CHAPTER ONE

GALLEONS, GUNS AND EAST INDIAMEN

In Europe, prior to the 16th century, ships were employed primarily for trade; in times of war, they were used simply to transport troops and materiel to land battles overseas. The ships of the Spanish Armada, for example, were mainly military transports, and were a poor match for the swifter and more manoeuvrable fighting ships that had been developed by the English.

The Spanish fleet was chased along the Channel, then up through the North Sea, and had to make its way back home by sailing in a wide circle around Scotland and Ireland. Here, it was exposed to the full force of the Atlantic gales, and in those unfamiliar and dangerous waters, many vessels came to grief. Of the 130 ships and 30,000 men that left Lisbon in May 1588, only 40 ships and around 10,000 men returned.

It was in the 16th century, during the reign of Henry VIII (1509–47), that the birth of English naval power was marked by the construction of a fleet of fighting ships armed with heavy guns, and the establishment of a naval administration. One of the trends that marked this era was the desire to build bigger and bigger ships that could carry ever larger numbers of guns, in the hope of being able to reduce an enemy's fleet to matchwood through sheer cannon power. But as so often with attempts at innovation, unforeseen problems frequently led to disaster and tragedy.

THE *MARY ROSE*, 1545

The *Mary Rose* was built at Portsmouth in 1509–10 and, along with her sister ship the *Great Harry*, was regarded as the flower of Henry VIII's fleet. She underwent a major refit in 1536 when her clinker hull was rebuilt with carvel planking. This technique, copied from the Portuguese caravel, produced a smooth hull and allowed the fitting of gun-ports, marking the transition from the old style of warship, which carried few guns, but large numbers of soldiers and archers for boarding enemy vessels, to the ship-of-the-line, which carried many guns to fire broadsides at the enemy.

It was during the Battle of Portsmouth, on 19 July 1545, that the *Mary Rose* met her tragic end. Under the command of Vice-Admiral Sir George Carew, and flanked by the *Great Harry*, she led the English fleet out of Portsmouth harbour to meet a French invasion force of over 200 vessels, watched from Southsea Castle by King Henry VIII himself. The great ships were ready for battle, their gun-ports open and decks crammed with fighting men. There was not much of a breeze, but the *Mary Rose* began to hoist more sail to make use of what little there was, when for some reason she began to heel over. What happened exactly will never be known, but it is thought that the initial list was caused by poor sail handling, and that this was exacerbated by hundreds of soldiers tumbling across the deck, followed by improperly secured guns. As all this weight shifted to one side of the ship, she tipped

Above and opposite: *Wind and weather inflicted more casualties on the Spanish Armada than the guns of the English fleet.*

> **It was in the 16th century, during the reign of Henry VIII, that the birth of English naval power was marked by the construction of a fleet of fighting ships armed with heavy guns, and the establishment of a naval administration.**

over even more until the lower gun-ports on the starboard side dipped beneath the water – the hold filled, and the great ship quickly sank to the bottom, leaving only the tops of her main- and foremasts projecting above the surface. Of the 700 men aboard, only 35 survived. Those on the gun-decks had no chance of escape, while the armoured soldiers sank like stones, and those on deck were entangled in the rigging and the anti-boarding nets.

The wreck of the *Mary Rose* was located by underwater archaeologists in the 1960s, and the remains of the ship (the keel and much of the starboard side) were raised in 1982. The preserved hull is now on display near *HMS Victory* in Portsmouth, along with an exhibition of the hundreds of fascinating items that were recovered during her excavation.

THE *TRYAL* (1622) AND THE *BATAVIA* (1628)

The danger and uncertainty facing the early navigators are well illustrated by the tale of the East Indiaman *Tryal*, the fate of which was to become the earliest recorded English wreck in Australian waters. Neither the ship's master, John Brooke, nor his mates had ever made the voyage to Batavia (now Djakarta) before, and they had to rely on the journal of another captain who had sailed there in 1620. The *Tryal* departed Plymouth on 4 September 1621, and put in at the Cape of Good Hope for supplies in March 1622. Brooke tried to engage the services of an experienced mate to act as pilot in the Indian Ocean, but without success, and the *Tryal* sailed from the Cape on 19 March with 143 persons on board.

Brooke sighted land on 1 May, believing it to be an island described in the previous captain's journal; in fact, it was the mainland of north-western Australia, south of Barrow Island. However, without a means of determining his longitude accurately, he was effectively lost. He set a course north-east towards where he thought the Sunda Strait should be, when in fact the proper course lay to the north-north-west. On 25 May, in fair weather and smooth seas, the *Tryal* struck the southern end of the Monte Bello Reef and began to fill rapidly. The

captain, his cabin boy and eight passengers hurriedly got into the skiff and abandoned the ship, much to the despair and disgust of those remaining. The first mate launched the longboat and took off another 36 people. Both boats sailed north and succeeded in reaching Batavia six weeks later, but of the 90 or so people left on the *Tryal*, nothing was ever seen or heard again.

The *Batavia*, a Dutch East Indiaman, suffered a similar fate, but the aftermath was far more grisly. She departed Texel Roads, Holland, on 27 October 1628, bound for Java with a cargo of general merchandise, cochineal and money, and a complement of 318 passengers and crew, including the fleet commander, François Pelsaert. She sailed at the head of a fleet of seven ships, but became separated in bad weather after replenishing stores at the Cape of Good Hope and continued alone. Discipline on board was poor, and there was animosity between the fleet commander and the captain, Ariaen Jacobsz.

On 4 June 1629, as Jacobsz stood his watch in the pre-dawn darkness, he thought he saw the white spray of breaking waves directly ahead, but dismissed it as a trick of the moonlight. However, his eyes had not been deceived, and within a few minutes the *Batavia* struck a reef near the Abrolhos Islands, off the coast of western Australia. Though stuck fast, the ship remained afloat for a week, and the crew was able to ferry passengers, supplies and water to a nearby island. Pelsaert, Jacobsz and 46 others then set sail in the longboat, exploring the mainland coast for water before heading north towards Java, 1,200 miles (1,930 kilometres) away; they were picked up four weeks later by a Dutch ship.

Pelsaert accused Jacobsz of losing the ship through negligence, putting him under arrest before setting out to rescue the remainder of the *Batavia*'s passengers and crew. He arrived at the Abrolhos Islands on 17 September and found, to his horror, that one Jeronimus Cornelisz had set himself up as a dictator, seizing the *Batavia*'s treasures and indulging in an orgy of rape and murder. Pelsaert, 'hoping to find a large party of people alive, had to learn with heart's grief that more than 120 persons, Men, Women and Children, had been Miserably

Opposite: The loss of the Dutch East Indiaman Batavia, wrecked off Western Australia in 1627, led to a terrible tale of misery and murder.

EAST INDIAMEN

'. . . More than 120 persons, Men, Women and Children, had been Miserably murdered, by drowning as well as by Strangling, Hacking and Throat-cutting.'

CHRONOMETER

The quest for a practical means of determining longitude at sea finally ended with the invention of a reliable marine chronometer, first achieved by John Harrison in 1759, but perfected by the Frenchman Pierre Le Roy.

murdered, by drowning as well as by Strangling, Hacking and Throat-cutting'. Forty people had drowned while abandoning ship, and another 20 had succumbed to illness, bringing the death toll to 185. Cornelisz and seven of his henchmen were hanged on the island, while two more were cast away on the mainland – the first recorded Europeans ever to live in Australia.

THE *VASA*, 1628

The *Vasa*, built in Stockholm's Royal Dockyard in 1627, was to be the Swedish equivalent of the *Mary Rose* – a huge warship with 64 guns on two decks. But, unlike Henry VIII's flagship, the finest vessel in the Swedish Navy never actually went to sea. The 1,300-ton (1,320-tonne) *Vasa*, 180 feet (55 metres) long and decorated with superbly carved wooden sculptures, foundered while leaving Stockholm harbour on her maiden voyage on 10 August 1628. Again, it seems that the ship was top-heavy. She had failed a stability test – 30 men running back and forth across the deck had caused her to roll dangerously – but political pressure forced her to sail regardless. As she lumbered majestically out of harbour, an initial heel brought on by a gust of wind dipped her lower gun-ports into the water, and she filled quickly and sank in an upright position. Of the 200 men on board, between 30 and 50 were drowned.

The wreck was discovered by divers in 1956, resting upright on the sea-bed and buried in mud up to the water-line. The low salinity and temperature

of Baltic sea water had protected the hull from attack by marine life, and the ship was in a remarkable state of preservation. She was raised in 1961, and is now on show in a specially constructed museum in Stockholm.

THE *ASSOCIATION, EAGLE, ROMNEY* AND *FIREBRAND*, 1707

The worst maritime disaster ever to occur in British waters unfolded on the evening of 22 October 1707, among the notorious Western Rocks of the Scilly Isles. A fleet of 21 British warships, under the command of Admiral Sir Cloudesley Shovell in the flagship *HMS Association*, had left Gibraltar on 27 September. During their homeward voyage, they had been battered by gales from several directions, and by the time they had crossed the Bay of Biscay they were hopelessly lost. The fleet hove to and took soundings, coming to the conclusion that they were off the island of Ushant at the western tip of Brittany. So, despite the poor visibility, they sailed on in a north-easterly direction, thinking that the English Channel lay ahead. But they were far to the north of their assumed position, and at around 8 pm on 22 October the *Association* ran on to the Gilstone Ledges, to the west of Scilly, and foundered with all hands. In the confusion, three other ships – the *Eagle*, *Romney* and *Firebrand* – also struck rocks and went down. Of the 1,673 men who had sailed on the four ships, only 26 survived; the body of the admiral was washed up on a beach on the southern side of St Mary's in the Scillies.

The loss of Admiral Shovell's ships caused a public outcry about the state of navigation in the Royal Navy and led indirectly to the passing of the Act of Longitude, which offered prizes of up to £20,000 (an incredible fortune in those days) for anyone who could come up with a practical and accurate means of finding longitude at sea. Ironically, it seems that longitude had nothing to do with the Scilly disaster of 1707. A subsequent examination of the compasses carried by the fleet showed that only three were serviceable, and the surviving logbooks indicated that no allowance had been made for magnetic variation on the voyage back from Gibraltar.

Right: *The wreck of the 17th-century Swedish warship* Vasa *was raised in 1961, and its magnificent carved timbers can now be admired in its own museum in Stockholm.*

Opposite: *The wreck of the* Association *and three other ships near the Scilly Islands in 1707 resulted in the greatest ever loss of life in British waters.*

CHAPTER TWO

THE AGE OF SAIL

Shipping was of fundamental importance to the politics and economy of the 18th and 19th centuries, sustaining trade with the New World, the Far East and Australia, and facilitating the expansion and administration of empire for all the colonial powers especially Great Britain.

The great sailing ships that plied the trade routes of the 19th century were the distillation of centuries of experience, and they were handled by men who were rooted in an age-old tradition of the sea. However, despite improvements in charts and navigation techniques, sailing ships were still at the mercy of wind and weather. There was scant regard for safety, and the huge losses of ships and lives that were suffered each year were scarcely given a thought by the general public. In the year 1852, 1,115 vessels and over 900 lives were lost around the shores of the United Kingdom alone. A single January gale, which lasted for five days, claimed 257 ships and 486 lives. The number of sailing vessels lost in British waters reached a peak in 1864 – 1,741 ships and 516 lives – as steam began to replace sail. The dangers were far greater, of course, in unfamiliar and poorly charted foreign waters, and in the stormy expanses of the oceans.

WRECK OF THE *LUTINE*, 1799

The futuristic Lloyd's Building in London is the latest home of the world-famous insurance association, which has been closely linked with the world of shipping since its beginnings in 1688. In the central atrium stands the famous *Lutine* bell, which is rung once to announce a total loss, and twice when a ship is posted missing. The bell was salvaged from the wreck of the *Lutine*, which foundered on the treacherous sandbanks between Vlieland and Terschelling in the Frisian Islands in 1799.

The *Lutine* began her life as *La Lutine*, a French 26-gun frigate launched at Toulon in 1779. She was surrendered to British forces under Admiral Hood during the siege of Toulon in 1793, and taken back to England to be refitted as a 32-gun frigate of the Royal Navy. At the beginning of October 1799, the *Lutine* was anchored in Yarmouth Roads with the rest of the North Sea Fleet, under Admiral Lord Duncan, when she was requisitioned to transport a large quantity of bullion to Hamburg. Her cargo included around £900,000 worth of gold and silver bars, and coins to the value of £300,000 – no small sum today, but at that time a veritable king's ransom. She set sail in the early hours of Wednesday, 9 October, under the command of Captain Lancelot Skynner RN, bound for Cuxhaven at the mouth of the Elbe.

The *Lutine*'s course took her north of the low-lying Frisian Islands, with their shifting sandbanks and dangerous currents. There, on the night of 9 October, she was hit by a north-north-westerly gale and found herself pinned against a lee shore. It seems that she was driven on to the sandbanks between Terschelling and Vlieland, and quickly broke up in the pounding surf. Captain Mortlock of the British ship *Wolverine*, lying in the lee of Vlieland, saw rockets in the night sky, but by the time he had organized rescue boats, the dawn revealed a wild sea littered with wreckage, chattels and corpses. Of the 240 crew on board, only one man survived, clinging to a piece of wreckage. The islanders buried around 200 corpses in a pit near the Brandaris lighthouse, while three of the ship's officers were interred in the churchyard in Vlieland.

Above: *The* Lutine *bell, recovered from the wreck of the* Lutine *in 1858, hangs in the atrium of Lloyd's of London and is rung to announce the loss of an insured vessel.*

Opposite: *This illustration to Faulkner's* The Shipwreck *of 1827, shows just how vulnerable sea-going vessels of the time were to sudden squalls and storms.*

SALVAGE OPERATION

A total of 99 gold and 101 silver bars were retrieved, plus around 58,000 gold and silver coins. The most famous relics are owned by Lloyd's of London, including the *Lutine*'s bell.

Right: *One of the many salvage operations on the wreck of the Lutine. This effort, in 1896, recovered a cannon and an anchor.*

With such a valuable cargo, salvage efforts began the following year and continued well into the 20th century, but only two efforts (in 1800 and 1858) were truly successful – a total of 99 gold and 101 silver bars were retrieved, plus around 58,000 gold and silver coins. The most famous relics, however, are possessed by Lloyd's – the *Lutine*'s bell and a table and chair carved from the ship's rudder. Both bell and rudder were recovered during the 1858 salvage operation.

THE *NEVA* (1835) AND THE *CATARAQUI* (1846)

King Island lies at the western entrance to Bass Strait, about half-way between Tasmania and mainland Australia. Its position at the mouth of the so-called 'Shipwreck Strait' – unlit, uninhabited and ringed by rocks – made it a graveyard for many of the convict and emigrant ships heading for Sydney in the early part of the 19th century.

The barque *Neva* departed Cork on 8 January 1835, bound for Sydney with nine emigrant passengers and a crew of 26; locked in her hold, in conditions of unimaginable squalor, were 155 female convicts and 55 children. The voyage was uneventful until the early hours of 14 May, when the ship was approaching the entrance to Bass Strait, with a west-north-west gale on her port quarter. At about 2 am, the deck watch sighted land ahead – King Island – and the ship altered course to the north until she was close-hauled on the port tack. Three hours later, breakers were seen directly ahead – the helm was put hard over, but her stern struck a rock, unshipping the rudder and leaving the *Neva* helpless. She struck again on the port bow and swung beam-on to the heavy seas, leaning over and pounding on the reef. The prison stanchions broke open, allowing the terrified women and children in the hold to swarm on to the deck in a panic, where many were washed overboard. The boats were lowered, but all were smashed on the rocks or capsized in the surf.

Four hours after striking the rocks, the *Neva* broke up and sank. Twenty-two people drifted ashore at King Island on fragments of floating wreckage, but after eight hours in the water, seven of them died of exposure. The survivors, who included the captain and first mate, met the crew of another shipwreck and scraped a living on the island for a month until they were picked up by a passing ship. Of the 240 people who left Cork, only 15 survived. A court of inquiry cleared the master of the *Neva*, attributing the wreck to strong tides setting the ship south of her estimated course and to poorly charted reefs.

Ten years later, convict transports had been replaced by emigrant ships, crammed with people hoping to start a new life in the colonies. One of these was the *Cataraqui*, which departed Liverpool on 20 April 1846 under Captain C.W. Finlay. She was carrying 369 emigrants (including 73 children), eight private passengers and a crew of 46. Again, the voyage was without incident until the *Cataraqui* was approaching the entrance to Bass Strait. She was hove to in a gale, and for the previous four days bad weather had prevented the captain from taking an observation of sun or stars to determine his position. Dead-reckoning put the ship about 100 miles west of King Island, and as the gale eased at 3 am on 4 August 1846, Captain Finlay ordered sail to be hoisted and the voyage resumed.

It was a fatal error not to wait for daylight. Only 90 minutes later the *Cataraqui* ploughed into a reef at the southern end of King Island. Many of the unfortunate emigrants drowned below decks in the scramble to escape the rapidly filling ship, and many more were swept from the deck by breaking seas. The ship broke up during the following afternoon, casting all the survivors into the waves. Only nine made it ashore to King Island, where they lived for five weeks with a party of seal hunters until a ship took them off to Hobson's Bay (now Melbourne). With 414 lives lost, the wreck of the *Cataraqui* still stands as Australia's worst ever maritime disaster.

THE EMIGRANT SHIP *ANNIE JANE*, 1853

The second half of the 19th century saw vast numbers of emigrants heading to North America – Scots evicted during the Highland Clearances, Russians, Germans and Scandinavians. The ships that carried them were often overcrowded, insanitary and poorly maintained, and conditions on

board must have been terrible. One such was the *Annie Jane*, which left Liverpool in September 1853, having returned there for repairs after losing her mizzen mast in severe gales a few weeks earlier. On board were 450 passengers and crew, mainly Scottish emigrants with a few Irish, French and Germans. She passed through the North Channel, between Rathlin Island and the Mull of Kintyre, and continued north-west, heading for the northerly route to North America, which was favoured by west-bound sailing ships, as it lay north of the east-flowing Gulf Stream and was much less likely to suffer headwinds.

But the night of 28 September found the *Annie Jane* struggling once again in wild weather, near the southern tip of the Hebrides. Off the island of Barra, she was struck by a huge breaking wave, which smashed in the poop deck, instantly crushing hundreds of the unfortunate emigrants. Mortally wounded, the ship began to break up in the mountainous seas, and in ten minutes she had sunk, save for a large fragment of decking, which was washed ashore with a number of exhausted survivors clinging to it. Of the 450 who had been aboard, 348 had perished in the waves.

FIRE AND CANNIBALISM ON THE *COSPATRICK*, 1874

The *Cospatrick* was a fine teak clipper, built in 1856 and measuring 190 feet overall. Commanded by Captain Emslie, she departed London on 11 September 1874, bound for Auckland with 433 emigrant passengers and 42 crew. Sixty-five days out, on the night of 17 November, the ship was approximately 300 miles south-west of the Cape of Good Hope. The passengers had just enjoyed a concert on deck and were retiring to their berths when smoke was spotted coming from the forepeak. The fire quickly spread to the waist of the ship, causing great panic, but the captain held off lowering the boats while his crew vainly fought to control the blaze. By the time the order to abandon ship was given, it was too late – the *Cospatrick* was an inferno, and only two small boats with about 60 people aboard managed to get away before the

remains of the burnt-out hulk and its human freight slipped beneath the waves.

The boats had neither food nor water and were soon separated by bad weather. One was never seen again, but the other was picked up after ten days by the *British Sceptre* of Liverpool. Only five people were still alive, and two of them died soon after being rescued. The three survivors, including the second officer, Henry Macdonald, told a horrific tale of how they had survived by eating the flesh of their dead shipmates. A total of 472 people had been lost, including 111 children and 16 infants under the age of 12 months.

THE LOSS OF THE *THOMAS W. LAWSON*, 1907

The American ship *Thomas W. Lawson* was the largest pure sailing vessel ever constructed, measuring 375 feet (114 metres) overall and registered at 5,218 tons (5,300 tonnes). Built in Boston in 1902, she was a steel-hulled ship rigged as a seven-masted schooner and could be handled by a crew of only 19 men, using steam-powered winches to haul the running gear – she carried 43,000 square feet of canvas, and her sails weighed a total of 18 tons. She was intended to show that sailing ships with small crews could be more practical and economical than dirty, coal-guzzling steamships.

She departed Philadelphia for London on 20 November 1907 with a cargo of 60,000 barrels of paraffin oil. After weathering two severe gales in mid-Atlantic she arrived off the Scilly Isles on Friday 13 December with only six usable sails left. She had been set to the north of her intended course and found herself amid the Western Rocks with too little sail to go about and not enough room to wear ship. With the weather worsening, she was anchored between Nuns Deeps and Gunners Ledge in Broad Sound, in the hope of riding out the north-westerly gale that had started to blow.

The giant schooner's plight had been noticed on shore and, as darkness approached, the St Agnes lifeboat went out and landed a local pilot on board, but it was soon forced to return by the rapidly deteriorating weather. By midnight, the wind had

Opposite: A contemporary engraving shows the handful of survivors of the Cospatrick *disaster as they sight the rescue ship* British Sceptre.

Right: The magnificent 4-masted barque Pamir, built in Germany in 1905, served as a sail training ship from 1955 until her disappearance in 1957.

increased to 90 mph (145 kph), and at 1.15 am the ship's anchor cables parted. Fifteen minutes later, the *Thomas W. Lawson* struck the Shag Rock broadside-on and broke in two. Her crew, who had climbed into the mizzen rigging, were flung into the water. Next day, in still dangerous seas, a six-oared gig set out from St Agnes to search for survivors, but only three were found. Seventeen had perished, including the pilot, whose eldest son had manned the rescue gig.

THE DISAPPEARANCE OF THE *PAMIR*, 1957

Although sail had largely been replaced by steam by the early part of the 20th century, large sailing ships were still being built and operated right up until World War 2. Two such were the *Pamir* and the *Passat*, built by the famous Blohm and Voss yard in Hamburg in 1905. These fine ships were steel-hulled, four-masted barques of around 3,100 grt (8,680 cubic metres), 275 feet (84 metres) long and able to set 5,000 square yards (4,180 square metres) of canvas. For many years, they sailed to the Pacific via Cape Horn, carrying grain from Australia and nitrates from Chile, until they were laid up in 1945. They were destined for the breaker's yard until a German consortium, the *Pamir-Passat* Foundation, rescued them in 1955 to serve as sail training vessels for the German merchant marine.

The *Pamir*'s last voyage began in late August 1957, when she departed Buenos Aires bound for Hamburg, under Captain Johann Diebitsch, on her 16th round trip as a training ship. She was carrying over 3,000 tons (3,050 tonnes) of barley and had on board 35 crew and 51 cadets aged between 16 and 18. The ship followed the old clipper route north through the Atlantic, sailing close-hauled through the north-east trades into the variable winds and frustrating calms of the horse latitudes. It was there, on 20 September, when she was 500 miles (800 kilometres) south-west of the Azores, that Captain Diebitsch received the first radio warning of Hurricane Carrie, then brewing near the Cape Verde Islands, over 1,500 miles (2,414 kilometres) to the south-east.

Most hurricanes build slowly as they drift west across the Atlantic, then curve north through the Caribbean, but a few rogue storms deepen quickly and track rapidly to the north-west; unfortunately for the *Pamir*, Carrie was a rogue. During the following day, the barometer plummeted, and the increasing wind and sea heralded the approach of heavy weather. Then, at 8 pm, came a radio warning that the hurricane would hit the square-rigger within a few hours. That evening, ships in the North Atlantic picked up a series of SOS messages from the *Pamir*; the final message read: 'Lost all sails. Beginning to list badly. Need help.' Several ships responded and steamed at full speed to the given position, but when they arrived around midnight, they found nothing but wild and wind-swept waves.

An air and sea search was mounted at first light next day, involving aircraft from the US Air Force base in the Azores, but all that could be found were a few empty lifeboats. Then, at dusk on 22 September, the American freighter *Saxon* found a swamped lifeboat containing five exhausted survivors. On the following day, another boat with one man was recovered, but that was all – the other 80 men and boys were lost.

The survivors told how their ship had been caught by the hurricane before they had the chance to take in sail. She had heeled right over until her canvas was torn to shreds, and it seems her cargo must have shifted, for she never righted again, even when the foremast was carried away. She had lain over at 30 degrees, then 40 degrees, battered by huge seas, until suddenly she capsized, flinging everyone into the sea. A few managed to cling to pieces of wreckage and scramble into boats that had floated free – it had been impossible to launch them with such a high angle of list – but most were sucked down with the ship or perished through cold and exhaustion.

It had been Captain Diebitsch's first voyage as master of the *Pamir*, and although he was a very experienced seaman, he had never been in command of a large square-rigged ship before – perhaps a more prudent skipper would have shortened sail earlier. It was also alleged that her cargo had not been stowed correctly: there had been a dockers' strike in Buenos Aires, and the cargo had been put aboard by army conscripts.

WINDSWEPT WAVES

Several ships responded to the *Pamir*'s SOS message, and steamed at full speed to the given position, but when they arrived, around midnight, they found nothing but wild and windswept waves.

CHAPTER THREE

THE AGE OF STEAM

In 1819, the Atlantic was crossed for the first time by a vessel equipped with a steam engine. But the *Savannah* was a full-rigged sailing ship equipped with collapsible paddle-wheels, which were powered by an engine that ran for only 85 hours during a crossing which lasted 85 days. Nevertheless, she pointed the way to the future.

By the 1840s there were regular steamer services across the Atlantic. Moreover, it was competition on this route that inspired advances in the speed and design of steam vessels over the next 100 years. The advent of steam engines made seafarers independent of the vagaries of the wind, but they were still exposed to the traditional hazards of bad weather, collision, poor navigation and human error, while the new-fangled boilers increased the dangers of fire and explosion.

THE DISAPPEARANCE OF THE *PRESIDENT*, 1841

By the middle of the 19th century, the North Atlantic sea route from Europe to North America was one of the busiest in the world, but it was a dangerous crossing, plagued by storms, poor visibility and icebergs drifting south from Arctic waters. The first casualty of the scheduled transatlantic run was the *President*, a wooden-hulled paddle-steamer belonging to the British and American Steamship Navigation Company. She was a new ship, built in 1840, and had made three transatlantic voyages, but she failed to inspire confidence in her master, ex-naval lieutenant Richard Roberts. Captain Roberts, who had gained notoriety a few years earlier after forcing the mutinous crew of the paddle-steamer *Sirius* to complete an Atlantic crossing at the point of a gun, declared his new charge to be a 'coffin ship'.

Nevertheless, the *President* departed New York on 11 March 1841, bound for Liverpool with 136 passengers and crew, including the music-hall comedian Tyrone Power (reputedly the grandfather of the Hollywood film star of the same name). She was never seen again, and the company went into liquidation soon afterwards.

THE LOSS OF THE *CITY OF GLASGOW*, 1854

The *City of Glasgow* was a ship of the Inman Line, launched in 1850, with a single screw powered by two steam engines. Her modern design had served her well over four years of plying the North Atlantic route. She had a top speed of 12 knots (21 kph), and she competed successfully with the older paddle-steamers. She left Liverpool on 1 March 1854, bound for Philadelphia with a full complement of 111 cabin and saloon passengers and 293 steerage passengers; her crew consisted of Captain Kenneth Morrison, four officers, a surgeon, a purser, four engineers, six firemen, five coal-trimmers, ten stewards, nine waiters, one stewardess, four quartermasters and 30 able-bodied seamen – in total, 480 persons.

At that time, a transatlantic passage normally took about 12 days in good conditions, but the only way of knowing that a ship had arrived safely was to wait until it (or another vessel) returned with news. (The first successful transatlantic telegraph cables were not laid until 1866.) But fears began to surface when it was reported that the *City of Glasgow* had not reached Philadelphia by 9 April, when the ship's owners wrote to *The Times* in an attempt to allay anxiety, saying, 'We believe the

Opposite: The President, *built in 1840, was typical of the early steamships that served the North Atlantic trade. She was also the first of many to disappear without trace.*

vessel to be detained in the ice on the banks of Newfoundland.' Her sister ship, the *City of Manchester*, had arrived in Liverpool on 17 March and reported that fields of icebergs had drifted much further south, and more thickly, than in previous years.

But nothing more was ever heard of the *City of Glasgow*. On 12 May, the *Glasgow Herald* newspaper reported that 'an almost general opinion is now entertained among the members of Lloyd's that the worst has befallen the noble vessel and her passengers and crew,' and she joined the long list of ships that have disappeared without trace in the North Atlantic.

THE *CENTRAL AMERICA*, 1857

Launched in 1853, in New York's East River, the US Mail Steamship Company's side-wheel steamer *Central America* was the mainstay of the monthly round trip from New York to Panama via Havana, picking up the West Coast mails, gold bullion from the Californian gold-fields, and deliveries of coins from the San Francisco Mint to the East Coast banks. At 9 am on Tuesday, 8 September 1857, she departed Havana bound for New York on her 43rd run. On board were 476 passengers, 102 crew and two million dollars' worth of gold and cash.

As the *Central America* steamed northwards between Florida and Grand Bahama, she was overtaken by a gale, which increased in strength over the next two days. By dawn on Friday, 11 September, she was caught in a full hurricane. Though strongly built of pine on oak frames, her seams began to work in the huge seas, and at 9 am the engineer reported that she was making water. By noon, the coal bunker floors were awash, and at 5.30 pm the water flooded the boiler fires, stopping the engines and the bilge pumps. The crew cut away the foremast and tried to set some sail astern in an attempt to keep her head up to the seas, but no canvas was strong enough and she began to wallow dangerously.

The next day, the wind abated slightly, but the ship was still making water. At noon, a sail was sighted and distress rockets were fired. The brig *Marine* responded and stood by while boats were lowered, 100 women and children being taken off before darkness fell. The *Marine* continued to stand by, but at 8 pm the *Central America* was overwhelmed by a huge wave and began to sink, going down stern first at an angle of 45 degrees with the helpless passengers still crowded on the deck. According to an eyewitness, 'The suction of the ship drew the passengers underwater for some distance, and threw them in a mass together . . . the struggle for life was intense with cries and shrieks for help . . . in ten minutes not less probably than 300 had sunk to rise no more.'

The following morning, the barque *Ellen* picked up 50 men, while another four were found nine days later by the British brig *Mary*, having drifted 476 miles (766 kilometres) without food or water. But 426 lives were lost, including that of the captain.

THE *ROYAL CHARTER* GALE, 1859

'Australia in under 60 days!' It was the proud boast of the Liverpool and Australia Steam Navigation Company that their magnificent steam clipper *Royal Charter*, held the record for the fastest passage to Melbourne, of only 59 days. Built in 1854 in Liverpool, she was 235 feet (72 metres) long, rigged for both sail and steam, and had accommodation for 500 passengers.

On 26 August 1859, the *Royal Charter* steamed out of Port Phillip Bay, homeward bound for Liverpool with a complement of 388 passengers and 112 crew. Many of the passengers were wealthy gold miners from Ballarat, heading back to the old country with the fruits of their labours: the ship's strong-room contained 68,397 ounces of gold (worth £273,000) and £48,000 in gold sovereigns. The voyage around the Horn and through the Atlantic was fast and uneventful, and early in the morning of 24 October, the *Royal Charter* hove to off Queenstown (now Cork) in Ireland after another record-breaking run of 55 days. Fourteen passengers were disembarked, along with letters and telegrams announcing the ship's safe arrival, before she continued north through St George's Channel. The passengers organized a little award ceremony for Captain Taylor and persuaded him to call in briefly at Holyhead so that they could see the *Great Eastern*, which at that time was the biggest and most famous ship in the world.

This short delay was to prove fatal. As the *Royal Charter* left Holyhead, then rounded the Skerries off the north-west point of Anglesey later that day, the barometer began to fall sharply. By 8 o'clock, a gale was blowing from the east, whipping up a steep sea and bringing fierce squalls and rain storms. The ship was off the north coast of Anglesey, a mere 50 miles (80 kilometres) from Liverpool, but was struggling to make headway against the strong winds and the now ebbing tide. The wind rose to Force 10, then Force 12 (over 70 mph/113 kph) and backed to the north; by 10.30 pm, the *Royal Charter* was trapped against a lee shore. Unable to hold her position against the hurricane, and being driven towards the land, Captain Taylor let go both anchors and fired off distress rockets, but the weather was too wild for any boat to put to sea.

In the early hours of 25 October, the anchor cables parted, and the engines were unable to hold the ship into the wind, despite the crew cutting down her three masts to reduce windage. Fifty yards (46 metres) from shore, between Moelfre Head and Lligny Bay, she struck a rock ledge. Sixty-foot (18-metre) waves swept over her, washing people from her decks and preventing the boats from being launched. At first light, a strong and courageous seaman managed to swim a line ashore through the surf, and a few people were taken off by breeches buoy, but at 7 am a huge wave crashed over the ship and she broke in two; an hour later, there was little left of her but twisted wreckage. The gruesome aftermath was later described in the *Illustrated London News*: 'The coast and fields above the cliffs were strewn with fragments of the cargo and of the bedding and clothing. Worse still, the rocks were covered with corpses of men and women frightfully mutilated, and strewn with the sovereigns the poor creatures had gone so far to seek . . .' Of the 498 people on board, no less than 459 were drowned, including Captain Taylor and all his officers.

The storm was a freak hurricane similar to the one that devastated southern Britain in October 1987. It became known as the '*Royal Charter* gale', and during a 24-hour period between 24 and 25 October, 195 vessels were wrecked around British

Opposite: *The loss of the* Royal Charter *in 1859 caught the imagination of the Victorian public, and many contemporary illustrations depicted her tragic end.*

33

shores. The wind remained above gale force for the next ten days, the storm claiming a total of 248 ships and 686 lives.

THE IOLAIRE TRAGEDY, 1919

It was New Year's Eve 1918. The war was over, and those who had survived its horrors were returning home. On the island of Lewis, in Scotland's Outer Hebrides, the womenfolk were preparing to welcome the lucky few who would be home in time for the traditional Hogmanay celebrations. Lewis, with a total population of only 30,000, had sent more than 6,000 men to the war, half of them serving in the Royal Naval Reserve; more than 300 were expected back on 31 December, having travelled by train from southern England to Kyle of Lochalsh.

The movements officer at Kyle had realized that the regular mail steamer, *Sheila*, would not be big enough to cope with the expected influx of men, so he requested the assistance of HM Armed Yacht *Iolaire*, based at Stornoway. The *Iolaire* was a 200-ton (203-tonne) steam yacht with an elegant clipper bow, built in Leith in 1881 and previously known as the *Amalthea*. When she arrived at Kyle, at 4 pm, her captain had a brief discussion with the movements officer, as the *Iolaire* had lifeboats for only 100, and lifejackets for 80, but she was expected to carry around 300 men. However, given the special circumstances, they decided to overlook the rule-book.

The trains began to arrive after 6 pm, and the men for Lewis were embarked: 60 were put aboard the *Sheila*, while 260 went on to the *Iolaire*. At 7.30 pm, the *Iolaire* cast off and headed north through the Inner Sound on the 60-mile (97-kilometre) crossing to Stornoway. It was a dark night with a clear sky, but around midnight, as the yacht forged ahead across the Minch, a fresh wind filled in from the south, bringing squalls of rain and whipping up a heavy sea. By 1.30 am on New Year's Day 1919, the *Iolaire* was approaching Stornoway harbour, now only a few miles distant. As she altered course to starboard to pass astern of the fishing boat *Spider*, which was chugging towards port at 5 knots (9 kph) – half the speed of the *Iolaire* – some of the men on the deck of the yacht began to feel a little uneasy.

These were fishermen with long experience of approaching their home port in all conditions, and they felt that the *Iolaire* had strayed too far to the east, but assumed that the officer on the bridge must have known what he was doing. Unknown to them, neither the captain nor his officers had ever entered Stornoway harbour at night.

At 1.55 am, red distress rockets were seen above the Biastan Holm rocks, just outside the entrance to Stornoway harbour. The *Iolaire* had struck the rocks and was leaning over to starboard, pounded heavily by the waves. Her decks and saloon were crowded with men, and there was a terrible crush as they tried to abandon ship. A boat was launched, but it was smashed against the ship's side. The hero of the night was John MacLeod, of Port of Ness, who managed to battle ashore with a heaving line, which enabled a hawser to be pulled over; by means of this, some 40 men made their way to the shore, while others struggled in the water. At around 3 am, there was an explosion as the ship broke her back and the funnel fell overboard, then she slipped off the rocks and sank. One man climbed the mast, which still protruded above the waves, and was rescued at 10 am the following morning.

But New Year's Day 1919 was a grim dawn for the people of Lewis. Word of the disaster had spread quickly, and distraught relatives gathered at Stornoway where the bodies had been laid out. 'It was a very sorrowful business for those who were waiting,' remembered Donald MacPhail, who was 17 at the time of the tragedy. 'As the bard said, "Home awaited them warm, and all was best prepared". All had been got ready – food and clothing for those who were expected, friendship and warmth, the families at home; then the awful news that they would never come . . .' Of the 284 men on board the *Iolaire*, 205 were lost on that terrible night; hardly a family on the island did not suffer a bereavement.

A Naval Court of Inquiry cleared the captain and officers of the *Iolaire* (all of whom drowned) of any blame. However, a Public Inquiry a month later found that the officer in charge did not exercise sufficient prudence, that he should have reduced speed rather than overtake the *Spider*, and that there were insufficient boats and lifebelts for the number of men on board.

Above: More than 200 servicemen from the island of Lewis lost their lives when the elegant steam yacht Iolaire, *commandeered by the Royal Navy, was wrecked off Stornoway on New Year's Day 1919.*

CHAPTER FOUR

PASSENGER LINERS

In 1839, Samuel Cunard and his partners established the first regular transatlantic steamship service, carrying mail and passengers between Liverpool, Halifax and Boston. When the US-owned Collins Line went into service in 1850, the competition for the fastest and most luxurious Atlantic crossing had begun.

But the greater the number of passengers carried on board a ship, the greater the potential loss of life if disaster should occur, and the great liners carried many hundreds of passengers. These bigger, faster ships were more difficult to manoeuvre and stop than their smaller predecessors, and in the days before radar, poor visibility was still a grave danger, a danger compounded by the commercial pressure on captains to make the fastest crossings possible. Collisions with icebergs and with other vessels would claim many lives during this period, including the 1,503 who died so needlessly in the most famous sea disaster of all – the sinking of the *Titanic*.

FIRE ON BOARD THE *AUSTRIA*, 1858

The scant regard given to safety in the early days of passenger ships is well illustrated by the case of the Hamburg-Amerika liner *Austria*. Built in 1857, she had a short and unlucky career that involved several breakdowns and engine repairs before she started on the transatlantic run in the following year. She departed Hamburg on 2 September 1858 and picked up more passengers at Southampton, bringing her complement to 538 including the crew. Nine days out of Southampton, the ship's surgeon decided that the steerage accommodation should be fumigated, and ordered a seaman to go below with a bucket of tar and a length of red-hot chain. The chain was to be dipped in the tar to make smoke, but the seaman dropped it and upset the bucket, setting the pitch on fire. Within minutes, the wooden bunks and bedding were ablaze, and the passengers poured out on deck in a panic, many jumping overboard immediately.

There were no officers on the bridge, and the terrified helmsman abandoned the wheel, allowing the ship to turn downwind, and the breeze to drive the flames and smoke along the deck. The engines could not be stopped, as the engineers had been suffocated by smoke, and the lead pipes that fed water into the fire-fighting pumps had melted with the heat. Finally, the magazine exploded and the *Austria* went down. Only one boat managed to get away, with 67 people on board, and it was picked up later by the French barque *Maurice*; the surgeon's rash decision had cost 471 lives.

THE WRECK OF THE *ATLANTIC*, 1873

The *Atlantic* was built in 1871 by Harland and Wolff, and she was one of the five original ships of the White Star Line (later to own the *Titanic*). She was 420 feet (128 metres) long, had a maximum speed of 14 knots (23 kph) and was regarded as one of the top passenger liners of her time. She departed Liverpool on 20 March 1873, bound for New York with 931 passengers and crew. It was a bad voyage right from the start, as the *Atlantic* battled head gales all the way across. After more than a week of slow progress and discomfort (the narrow-beamed ship rolled sickeningly in a heavy sea), and with the coal bunkers rapidly emptying, Captain J.A. Williams decided to alter course and head for the nearer port of Halifax, Nova Scotia.

Opposite: The French barque Maurice stands by helplessly while the German liner Austria goes up in flames. Only 67 of the 538 people on board survived.

There were no officers on the bridge, and the terrified helmsman abandoned the wheel, allowing the ship to turn downwind.

It was a poor decision. She was now nearing a dangerous and unfamiliar coast, and the bad weather had prevented her officers from obtaining an accurate position by observing the sun or stars; they were relying on dead-reckoning which, after several days of adverse winds and currents, could not be relied upon. At 3 am on 1 April, the *Atlantic* was steaming full ahead in pitch darkness when she ran into rocks off Meagher Island, Nova Scotia. The ship was crowded and panic set in immediately as she leaned over on the reef, battered by wind and waves. The boats were washed from the decks and smashed on the rocks, but one of the officers managed to swim a line to a dry rock 150 yards (137 metres) away. Many people were hauled to safety, but hundreds more succumbed to exposure and exhaustion and were swept away. As dawn lightened the sky, the local islanders came out in fishing boats to pick up survivors, but no less than 560 lives had already been lost.

THE COLLISION OF *LA BOURGOGNE* AND THE *CROMARTYSHIRE*, 1898

The French liner *La Bourgogne*, of the Compagnie Générale Transatlantique, departed New York on Saturday, 2 July 1898, bound for Le Havre with 711 passengers and crew on board. By Sunday night, poor navigation had put her 160 miles (260 kilometres) to the north of her proper course and, despite darkness and thick fog, she was steaming eastwards at full speed, about 60 miles (100 kilometres) to the south of Sable Island, off Nova Scotia.

Meanwhile, the British sailing ship *Cromartyshire* was westward bound from Dunkirk to Philadelphia with a cargo of coal. At around 5 am on Monday, 4 July, the two ships met in the fog – the *Cromartyshire* struck the starboard side of *La Bourgogne* abreast of the engine room, hitting with such force that her foremast and main top-gallant mast were carried away, and most of her bows were torn off. *La Bourgogne* was steaming at such speed that she kept moving after the collision and disappeared into the murk.

The French captain decided to steam north towards Sable Island and try to beach his crippled ship in shallow water, but the boilers soon flooded and stopped the engines, leaving her to wallow in a heavy swell. The passengers, mostly Italian immigrants returning to Europe to visit relatives, began to panic and fight among themselves and with the crew as they rushed to the boats, while a small party of priests tried to calm things down. One boat full of women and children got away, only to be crushed by the falling funnel, while others were swamped or smashed against the ship's side; survivors later reported that crew members were pushing passengers overboard in their struggle for places in the boats. By the time *La Bourgogne* went down, only a couple of boats had got clear away, and 546 people were drowned. Of the 165 survivors, only one was a woman – no less than 104 were crew.

Though badly damaged, the *Cromartyshire* stayed afloat and managed to pick up the survivors from *La Bourgogne*. She was eventually found by the liner *Grecian* and towed safely into Halifax harbour.

THE SINKING OF THE *TITANIC*, 1912

Wireless operator John Phillips tapped out the historic message a second time: 'SOS. We have struck iceberg. Require assistance. Position 41.46N 50.14W. *Titanic*.' It was approaching midnight on Sunday, 14 April 1912, and the world's most notorious sea disaster had just begun to unfold.

The White Star Line's *Titanic* was the largest and most luxurious liner in the world, and a floating symbol of her era. She was a masterpiece of heavy engineering: 852 feet (260 metres) long, with a beam of 92.5 feet (28 metres), and a gross registered tonnage of 46,329 (129,721 cubic metres). Her huge triple-expansion steam engines delivered a cruising speed of 22 knots (41 kph). She represented the triumph of technology over the forces of nature, and the claim that she was unsinkable exemplified the overweening confidence of her makers.

She began her maiden voyage from Southampton just after noon on Wednesday, 10 April 1912, picking up passengers at Cherbourg and Queenstown (now Cork) before pointing her bows westward into the North Atlantic. She was carrying 1,316 passengers – 606 in first and second class,

Above: *The tragic fate of the* Titanic *inspired countless books, plays, films, paintings and musical works of widely varying merit.*

Opposite: *An artist's impression of the White Star liner* Atlantic *aground on Meagher Island, Nova Scotia, in 1873. 560 lives were lost in the disaster.*

Above: Hundreds of people perished in the freezing waters while those lucky enough to find a place in a lifeboat waited to be rescued.

710 in steerage – and 892 officers and crew under the command of Captain Edward J. Smith. The first few days of the voyage were uneventful, with fine, clear weather and a calm sea. But on Sunday, 14 April, as the *Titanic* approached the Newfoundland Banks, the deck officers felt a chill in the air that signalled their approach to the cold, iceberg-laden waters of the Labrador Current. However, the captain did not order a reduction in speed – it was the ship's maiden voyage and his last, and there was subtle pressure to deliver a fast crossing. Visibility was good and, he reasoned, any iceberg big enough to do damage would be seen in time to avoid it.

Soon after 11.30 pm on Sunday night, the forward lookout signalled the bridge that an iceberg lay directly ahead. The first officer ordered the helmsman to 'starboard his helm' (a nautical expression that dates from the days of tiller steering – putting the helm to starboard causes the ship to alter course to port). He also ordered the engines astern and pulled the switch that closed the automatic doors in the watertight bulkheads. But a ship the size of the *Titanic* takes time to respond to the helm, and her bows came around with agonizing slowness as the iceberg loomed menacingly out of the darkness. She narrowly avoided a head-on collision, but a long, excruciating judder ran through the ship as she scraped along a ledge of ice below the waterline on the starboard side.

This grazing nature of the collision was one of the many ironies of the *Titanic* disaster – if the ship had struck the iceberg head-on, she would very probably have survived, as she was designed to float with up to four of her 15 watertight compartments flooded. As it was, the hull was ruptured through six of the compartments, and icy sea-water began flooding the forward holds and boiler rooms. A quick survey undertaken by the ship's architect, Thomas Andrews, confirmed the worst – she was settling by the head and would sink within an hour or two. Captain Smith told the radio operator to call for assistance, and instructed his officers to ready the lifeboats.

The story of what happened next has passed into legend, and has been told and retold in countless books and films – the shortage of lifeboats (there

Below: *The* Titanic *was effectively a floating hotel. Of her crew of almost 900, more than 500 were employed solely in looking after the passengers.*

THE CARPATHIA

The *Carpathia* steamed as fast as she could towards the scene, but by the time she arrived at 3.30 am, the *Titanic* had gone to the bottom.

Right: *This famous painting by C. J. Ashford captures the horror of the night of 14 April 1912, when hundreds perished in the freezing waters.*

was space for only 1,178 in the boats, and a total of 2,208 people on board); the doors from steerage that remained locked until the first-class passengers had been put on the boats; the band playing as the ship went down; and the ship *Californian* hove to amid the ice almost within sight of the *Titanic*, her wireless switched off and the stricken liner's distress rockets dismissed as celebratory fireworks.

The Cunard liner *Carpathia*, which had been 58 miles (93 kilometres) away when she received the distress call, steamed as fast as she could towards the scene, but by the time she arrived at 3.30 am, the *Titanic* had gone to the bottom. All that remained were the boats full of shocked and shivering survivors, and a calm sea littered with hundreds of floating corpses. In all, 705 people survived; 1,503 died, including Captain Smith, the first officer and all the engineers.

The *Titanic* disaster resulted in the first International Convention for Safety of Life at Sea, held in London in 1913, which established regulations requiring ships to provide lifeboat accommodation for everyone on board; to hold regular lifeboat drills; and to maintain a 24-hour radio watch. Unfortunately, even these new rules could do nothing to prevent the fate of the passengers and crew on the *Empress of Ireland*, only two years later.

Below: The sinking of the White Star liner Titanic in April 1912 grabbed the newspaper headlines around the world.

THE COLLISION OF THE *EMPRESS OF IRELAND* AND THE *STORSTAD*, 1914

With a length of 550 feet (168 metres) and a top speed of 18 knots (33 kph), the *Empress of Ireland* was the pride of the Canadian Pacific Railway Company's fleet. She was built in Glasgow in 1906 and had plied the transatlantic route for eight years when she departed from Quebec bound for Liverpool at 4.30 pm on Thursday, 28 May 1914. The great liner moved off down the St Lawrence River, with Captain Henry George Kendall in command, and a complement of 1,475 passengers and crew. She stopped briefly at Rimouski to pick up the mail, then continued down river; shortly after 1.30 am, the captain sighted the lights of an approaching ship, one point on the starboard bow and about 2 miles (3 kilometres) distant.

A minute later, the lights disappeared as a fog bank rolled across the river. As a precautionary measure, Captain Kendall put his engines full astern and sounded three short blasts on his whistle (the international signal that means 'My engines are going astern'), and the other ship answered with a single long blast ('I am making way through the water'). When he judged that the *Empress* had stopped, the captain sounded two long blasts (meaning 'I am under way, but not making way', i.e. stopped, but not anchored). Again, the other ship answered with a single blast. (When two ships are approaching each other in a channel, the 'Rules of

the Road' stipulate that they should pass each other 'port to port' – equivalent to driving on the right. They also require that, in poor visibility, vessels should proceed at 'a safe speed' and be prepared to reduce speed or stop if a fog signal is heard ahead of the beam.)

Two minutes after hearing the other vessel's signal, and expecting her to pass to port, Captain Kendall was horrified to see her lights looming out of the fog on his starboard side, only a ship's length away. He immediately ordered 'full ahead', but there was to be no escape – the 6,000-ton (6,096-tonne) Norwegian collier *Storstad* ploughed into the liner amidships, gouging a huge hole along her starboard side. As the ice-cold waters of the St Lawrence River poured into the ruptured hull, the captain kept his engines full ahead in a valiant attempt to run her into shallow water, but within a few minutes the boilers were flooded and the *Empress* lost power. As the radio operator sent out a mayday, Captain Kendall calmly told his officers, 'The ship is gone; women to the boats.'

The ship was already listing badly, and the decks were swarming with terrified passengers, some of whom leapt from the rail into the freezing water wearing only their night-clothes. Although the *Empress of Ireland* carried enough lifeboats for 2,000 persons, the ship was so badly damaged that there was no time to get them away. The crew managed to lower nine boats following the order to abandon ship, but the *Empress* turned over and

Above: The Empress of Ireland *sank only 14 minutes after being struck by the* Storstad. *Local boatmen had the unpleasant task of recovering the bodies.*

Opposite: *Although the* Empress of Ireland *carried more than enough lifeboats for all her passengers and crew, there was not enough time to launch more than a few.*

sank only 14 minutes after the collision. Hundreds of passengers were crushed and killed by the impact of the *Storstad's* bow, and many more must have drowned in their cabins. Captain Kendall was catapulted from the bridge as the ship turned turtle and was picked up by one of the lifeboats.

Meanwhile, Captain Andersen of the *Storstad* had seen the stricken liner disappear into the fog, and was of the opinion that it was his own ship that was in danger of sinking. However, although her bows were badly mangled, the worst of the damage was above the water-line, and later she was able to limp up river to dock at Montreal. Soon the crew of the *Storstad* began to hear the cries of the passengers who had escaped the sinking *Empress*, and the captain ordered all his boats lowered to pick up survivors, assisted by the *Eureka* and the *Lady Evelyn* from Rimouski, where the SOS message had been picked up. The rescue boats probed cautiously through the fog, finding the calm water littered with corpses and debris. They picked up hysterical and weeping survivors, many of whom were in shock and suffering from exposure. In all, 397 were saved, but a chilling total of 1,078 lives were lost that night. (Among the survivors from the *Empress of Ireland* was Frank Tower, an oiler and stoker. Better known as 'Lucks' Tower, he also survived the *Titanic* and the *Lusitania* disasters.)

A Court of Inquiry, headed by Lord Mersey (who also headed the inquiries into the *Titanic* and *Lusitania* sinkings), found the *Storstad* to be the cause of the collision; however, a Norwegian Maritime Court later cleared Captain Andersen of blame. Public confidence was deeply shaken by another major disaster so soon after the *Titanic*. Both sinkings occurred in calm seas in poor visibility. The *Titanic* remained afloat for hours, but suffered from a shortage of lifeboats; the *Empress* carried more than enough boats, but the crew didn't have time to launch them. Among the many suggestions made following the loss of the *Empress of Ireland* were calls for the design of a 'life-saving suit' and the invention of 'a light-ray that will penetrate a fog'. Of more immediate use was the proposal to introduce traffic separation schemes in restricted waterways.

Opposite: *The* Andrea Doria *continued to float for 11 hours after her collision with the* Stockholm, *allowing all those who survived the impact to escape safely.*

COLLISION OF THE *ANDREA DORIA* AND THE *STOCKHOLM*, 1956

On 25 July 1956, the luxury Italian liner *Andrea Doria* was steaming at her full speed of 23 knots (43 kph) towards the east coast of the USA. She was close to completing her 51st transatlantic crossing, having enjoyed fine summer weather on the voyage from Genoa, and Captain Pietro Calamai expected to make New York on time at 9 am the following morning. At around 3 pm, the ship ran into fog off the Massachusetts coast, and by evening, visibility had been reduced to half a mile. The captain continued at a very slightly reduced speed – he still wanted to arrive on time – and kept a careful watch on the radar. At 10.40 pm, a blip was seen, bearing four degrees on the starboard

bow, range 17 miles (27 kilometres), and moving east, directly in line with the *Andrea Doria*. The second officer estimated that the other vessel would pass about a mile (1.6 kilometres) to starboard; nevertheless, the captain ordered the helm to alter course four degrees to port.

A few minutes after 11 pm, when the *Andrea Doria* was about 45 miles (72 kilometres) south-east of Nantucket Island, lights were sighted through a break in the fog, about a mile (1.6 kilometres) away on the starboard bow: it was the Swedish liner *Stockholm*. What happened next is not clear, as the two captains provided conflicting accounts of the accident, but at 11.10 pm, the *Stockholm* struck the *Andrea Doria* on the star-board side, just forward of the bridge. Within minutes, the Italian ship had developed an 18-degree list, and SOS signals were sent out. The French liner *Ile de France* and several other ships answered, and between them they took off safely around 1,600 passengers and crew; 45 passengers died on the *Andrea Doria*, and five crew on the *Stockholm*, all as a result of the impact. At 10.09 am on 26 July, just an hour after she should have berthed at New York, the *Andrea Doria* went to the bottom.

In 1964, a salvage team attempted to retrieve the safes that had been on board the *Andrea Doria* (many of the passengers were very wealthy, and the liner had a casino), but all they managed to bring back was a bronze statue of the 16th-century Genoese admiral, Andrea Doria, after whom the ship had been named. It now stands in the foyer of a Florida motel.

CHAPTER FIVE

WARSHIPS AND SUBMARINES

The worst disasters at sea (in terms of lives lost) have all occurred during wartime when massive movements of troops and materiels have necessitated the crowding of the world's oceans. Safety considerations are primarily geared to avoiding the enemy and gaining port, and so natural hazards such as icebergs, hurricanes and fog have resulted in greater losses of crew and passengers.

The biggest ever loss of life on a single vessel took place when the German liner *Wilhelm Gustloff* was torpedoed by a Soviet submarine off Danzig in 1945. It was crammed with retreating troops and refugees, and an estimated 7,500 people were killed. In peacetime, military vessels have been as susceptible as other ships to the ordinary dangers of the sea, and often have had to cope with the added hazards of potentially explosive cargoes and new and un-tested designs.

THE *BIRKENHEAD*, 1852

The eighth Kaffir War was the most costly episode in the 100-year conflict between the Cape colonists and the Xhosa peoples of southern Africa. At the height of the war, the 1,400-ton (1,422-tonne) *Birkenhead*, a steam-auxiliary transport built in 1845, was converted to a troopship to carry reinforcements to the Cape. On 7 January 1852, she departed Queenstown in Ireland, carrying a crew of 130, plus 479 private soldiers and NCOs, 12 officers, three surgeons, 25 women and 31 children. She arrived at Cape Town in mid-February. Having disembarked invalids and taken on water, stores and horses, she set sail again on 25 February for Port Elizabeth in fine weather.

Less than 100 miles (161 kilometres) out, at 1.50 am on 26 February, she was steaming at 8 knots (15 kph) when the man on the lead-line reported a depth of only 12 fathoms (22 metres) off Danger Point. Alarmed, the officer-on-watch ordered another cast of the lead, but before this could be done, the ship ran on to an uncharted rock. Water rushed in and overwhelmed the lower troop decks, drowning hundreds of soldiers as they slept, but in an admirable display of discipline, the men on deck formed ranks and kept order while the boats were lowered. There were only eight boats (not nearly enough for all on board) – three got away, but a fourth was smashed by the toppling funnel as the stricken vessel rolled in the swell. The horses were driven off to swim ashore, but the poor creatures were attacked by sharks. Within 25 minutes of striking, the ship began to break up and sink.

The soldiers remaining on deck went down in good order – only three men broke ranks – before being pitched into the water, where many were attacked by the sharks that had been feasting on the horses. More than 60 made it to shore on floating wreckage, and another 40 were rescued from the rigging the next day; in all, 193 lives were saved, including those of all the women and children. Afterwards, Queen Victoria commissioned a memorial in the Chelsea Hospital, London, in honour of the gallantry and discipline of the 445 who died on the *Birkenhead*.

Above: More than 7,000 troops and refugees died when the German liner Wilhelm Gustloff *was sunk by a Soviet submarine in 1945.*

Opposite: Although 445 lives were lost in the wreck of the Birkenhead, all the women and children on board were saved.

THE CAPSIZE OF HMS *CAPTAIN*, 1870

The late 19th century was a time of radical change in the design of warships, with the move from sail to steam, the adoption of iron hulls and armour-plating, and a lively debate on the relative merits of the old-fashioned broadside versus turret-mounted guns. During this period, many clumsy, compromise vessels of doubtful stability were built; one of these was the ill-fated *Captain*.

Designed by retired naval officer Captain Cowper Coles, the 335-foot-long (102-metre) *Captain*, launched in 1870, had an iron hull with a full, three-masted sailing rig and twin, steam-driven screws. She had two revolving gun turrets on a low-slung gun-deck (with only 6 feet/2 metres of freeboard), a raised forecastle and quarter-deck, and a single funnel amidships. She behaved reasonably well during her first few months of service, although her officers were wary of her low freeboard. She was part of a squadron crossing the Bay of Biscay when the ships were caught in a gale on 6 September 1870. As night fell, the *Captain* was seen to be heeling excessively, and by daylight the following morning, she had disappeared.

The 18 survivors who were picked up told how a squall had hit the ship soon after midnight while the crew was shortening sail. The *Captain* lay right over to starboard and did not come up again, capsizing in a matter of minutes; 483 seamen were drowned, including her unfortunate designer.

The Court Martial following the loss of the *Captain* found that the ship was unstable and was '. . . built in deference to public opinion as expressed in Parliament and other channels, and in opposition to the views and opinions of the Controller of the Navy'.

THE LOSS OF *HMS VICTORIA*, 1893

The true reason for the tragic loss of the *Victoria*, flagship of the Royal Navy's Mediterranean Fleet, and the lives of 358 of her sailors will never be known, as the admiral who gave the order for the fatal manoeuvre went down with his ship. The fleet was steaming towards Tripoli in two columns, headed by the battleships *Victoria* (Admiral Sir George Tryon) and *Camperdown* (Rear-Admiral Hastings Markham), and as the ships approached the anchorage, Tryon signalled the two columns to make 180-degree turns towards each other (i.e. the port column turned to starboard, and the starboard column to port), preserving the order of the fleet.

Markham was taken aback, as there were only 6 cables (1,200 yards/1,097 metres) of sea-room between the two columns, and the normal turning circle allowed for such manoeuvres was 4 cables (i.e. 10 cables of sea-room would be needed to preserve minimum separation of 2 cables after completion of the turn). He ordered his flag-lieutenant to query the signal, but was cut short by a further signal from the admiral asking what he was waiting for.

Trusting that Admiral Tryon knew what he was doing – he had a reputation as a skilled and highly experienced tactician with a fondness for complicated manoeuvres – Markham acknowledged the signal, and the two battleships started to turn towards each other. Within minutes, it became obvious that a collision was going to take place. Admiral Tryon put the *Victoria*'s engines astern and ordered the watertight bulkhead doors closed, just as the *Camperdown* struck her on the starboard bow, about 10 feet (3 metres) abaft the hawse pipe. In those days, battleships were built with underwater rams projecting from the bow beneath the water-line, and the *Camperdown*'s ram did an effective job of penetrating the *Victoria*'s hull. The crippled flagship rapidly filled with water, lay over on her starboard side and capsized before going down by the head. The *Camperdown* was barely damaged, but only 284 of the *Victoria*'s 642 officers and crew escaped.

It seems likely that Admiral Tryon, for all his experience, made a simple mistake. While 180-degree turns are relatively uncommon in fleet manoeuvres, 90-degree turns (for which only 2 cables of sea-room are required) are often made, and the admiral perhaps forgot that extra sea-room was required for the half-circle turn. A lieutenant who had been on the bridge of the *Victoria* at the time of the collision later confided to Admiral Mark Kerr: 'That was exactly the reason. The admiral himself told me that that was the mistake he had

Opposite: Only 18 of the 501 officers and men on board HMS Captain survived the disaster.

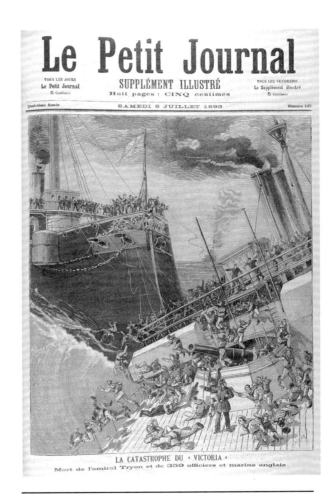

LA CATASTROPHE DU « VICTORIA »
Mort de l'amiral Tryon et de 359 officiers et marins anglais

Above: The front page of Le Petit Journal for Saturday 8 July 1893 reports the fatal collision between HMS Camperdown and HMS Victoria.

made. I could not make up my mind what I would do if I was called as a witness (at the subsequent Court Martial), for we had all been told . . . that we were to do everything to preserve Sir George's reputation . . . but fortunately I was not called to give evidence.'

EXPLOSION ON *HMS VANGUARD*, 1917

The dangers of carrying large quantities of high explosive on board are borne out by the numbers of large ships that exploded in harbour during World War 1. Four Italian, two Japanese, one Russian and four British warships were lost in this way, including the Dreadnought-class battleship *HMS Vanguard.*

The *Vanguard*, built in 1909, was 536 feet (163 metres) long, displaced 19,250 tons (19,558 tonnes) and had served with the Grand Fleet at the Battle of Jutland. On 9 July 1917, she was at anchor in the great natural harbour of Scapa Flow, in the Orkney Islands, when she was destroyed by a huge explosion. Of the 670 men on board, only one officer and two seamen survived, although later the officer died of his wounds. The resulting inquiry found that the explosion had probably been caused by the deterioration of the high explosives stored in her magazine.

THE WORLD'S WORST NAVAL PILE-UP, 1923

One of the most embarrassing events in the history of the US Navy was the pile-up that took place off southern California on 8 September 1923. A flotilla of seven destroyers – the USSs *Delphy*, the *Young*, the *Chauncey*, the *Fuller*, the *Nicholas*, the *Woodbury* and the *S.P. Lee* – under the command of Captain Edward H. Watson, had been taking part in manoeuvres and was steaming in line ahead, some 40 miles (64 kilometres) offshore. Despite being in thick fog, their commander assumed he had plenty of sea-room and was clear of hazards, and the flotilla was travelling at 20 knots (37 kph). Without warning, the *Delphy* ploughed into rocks near the tiny island of Santa Barbara, about 40 miles (64 kilometres) south-west of Santa Monica Bay.

The following ships had no time to stop or even reduce speed. The *Young* and the *Chauncey* smashed into the stern of the *Delphy*, while the other four ships ran on to the rocks on each side. All seven destroyers were total wrecks, and 22 of the 500 officers and men lost their lives.

During the subsequent inquiry, various excuses were put forward, including the effects of unusual currents and tides caused by the great earthquake that had devastated Yokohama and Tokyo the previous week, but in the end, it seems to have been a case of sloppy navigation and insufficient care.

HMAS VOYAGER (1964) AND USS FRANK E. EVANS (1969)

The Australian aircraft carrier *HMAS Melbourne* was involved in two fatal collisions in the space of five years. On the night of 10 February 1964, while on Australian Navy manoeuvres off Jervis Bay in New South Wales, she collided with the destroyer *HMAS Voyager*, resulting in the loss of 82 lives.

Five years later, the *Melbourne* was taking part in an international exercise in the South China Sea, about 650 miles (1,046 kilometres) south-west of Manila. At 3.15 am on 3 June 1969, she ran down the American destroyer *USS Frank E. Evans*, cutting the smaller ship in two. The bow section quickly sank, taking 74 sailors down with it, but the larger stern section was lashed alongside the *Melbourne* and 199 men taken off alive. The aircraft carrier suffered damage to her flight deck and bows, but was able to steam to Singapore for repairs.

Left: The aircraft carrier HMAS Melbourne, *her bows badly damaged after her collision with an American destroyer, being repaired.*

H.M.S. "VANGUARD"

Left: When the Vanguard *exploded only three men survived, although one died of his injuries later.*

enclosed hulls are extremely seaworthy, and they can escape bad weather simply by diving beneath the waves – but their cramped quarters, dependence on limited air supplies while submerged, and the difficulty of escape make them especially vulnerable in the event of fire or power loss. On the surface, there is still the danger of collision, and it was just such an accident that led to the world's worst ever submarine disaster, when the French submarine *Surcouf* was run down by an American freighter in the Caribbean in 1942. The *Surcouf* was a massive boat of 4,218 tons (4,285 tonnes) submerged displacement; her deck carried a turret with two 8-inch (20-centimetre) guns and a hangar containing a seaplane and a 16-foot (5-metre) boarding launch. When she went down, she took all 159 submariners with her.

Britain's worst submarine accident took place in Liverpool Bay in 1939. *HMS Thetis* had recently completed building, and on 1 June 1939 she headed down the Mersey for her first diving trials. On board was her normal crew of five officers and 48 men, but on this occasion, an extra 50 people, including civilian experts as well as naval personnel, were crammed into her cramped hull. As soon as she began to dive, her skipper knew something was not right – the bow seemed too buoyant. So as the dive continued, he sent an officer forward to check the torpedo tubes, which ought to have been flooded. There were ten tubes, and one to four were dry, so the officer went on to number five. He made the standard checks before opening the inner door: first, he noted that the bow cap indicator was in the closed position; then he opened the test-cock, a narrow pipe containing a tap that lets water trickle through if the tube is flooded. There was no water from the test cock, so he opened the tube's inner door – and thousands of gallons of water came flooding into the torpedo room.

Unable to close the door against the pressure, the officer struggled aft with the water level rising around his knees, and managed to close the watertight door at the second bulkhead. This contained the flooding, but the now bow-heavy submarine dived down and buried her head in the soft mud of the sea-floor, 160 feet (50 metres) below the surface. The ballast tanks were blown,

Above: *The giant French submarine* Surcouf *was run down by an American freighter in 1942; all of the 159 submariners on board were killed.*

Opposite: *The stern of the crippled submarine HMS Thetis pokes above the waves, as rescuers attempt to save the 99 men still trapped inside.*

SUBMARINE DISASTERS

Ever since submarines first began to be developed seriously, at the beginning of the 19th century, there has been a steady stream of accidents. These have often been due to the many novel design problems that must be dealt with in the development of a completely new type of vessel, but many have been caused by human error. Submarines are not affected by some of the dangers faced by other ships – their

but the 275-foot (84-metre) vessel assumed a position with her bows on the mud and her stern just clearing the surface.

By now, it was evening, and a search for the overdue submarine had begun. Meanwhile, the captain had decided to wait until dawn before putting people out through the escape hatches, as there was no sign of a rescue boat having arrived and escapees would probably die of exposure if they were not picked up immediately. The crippled sub was reached by the destroyer *HMS Brazen* at 6.30 am, and by 8 am the first two men reached the surface via the escape hatch. But the air in the sub was already foul, and time was running out for those still trapped. It took 30 minutes to blow the water from the escape chamber each time it was used, and after the first exit, the inner hatch was opened too soon, allowing a few gallons of water to pour into the hull. This flowed forward and shorted electrical equipment, causing a small fire which, though swiftly extinguished, consumed a lot of precious oxygen.

Painfully aware that oxygen was fast running out, the officer in charge squeezed four people into an escape chamber designed for two, but when the outer hatch did not open and the chamber was drained, there were three dead men inside and a fourth near to death. They tried again with two men, who reached the surface alive at 10 am, but they were the last to escape. Time had run out for the 99 men still inside the *Thetis*. Eventually, the submarine was salvaged and refitted. Renamed *Thunderbolt*, she served in World War 2 until she was sunk by an Italian ship with the loss of a further 63 lives.

Investigators later found that the bow cap indicators on *Thetis* did not all point in the same direction when closed – the normal arrangement on earlier submarines. The test-cock pipe was blocked by fresh paint. Following the *Thetis* disaster, the Royal Navy adopted the American 'free ascent' system of submarine escape, and built a 100-foot (30-metre) training tower at HMS *Dolphin* in Portsmouth for instruction in this technique. They also recommended the introduction of a standing organization for search and rescue to improve the dismally slow response time to the emergency.

CHAPTER SIX

FERRIES AND RIVERBOATS

The relatively sheltered waters in which ferries and riverboats operate protect them from many of the dangers of the open ocean, but they must face the special hazards of navigating in shallow waters and crowded sea-lanes busy with traffic.

In the Dover Strait, for example, over 200 ferry crossings are made daily in summer, and the ferries must weave a safe route across the path of the 300 or so cargo ships and tankers that pass through the narrow channel each day. Ferries are also subject to commercial pressure to carry as many paying customers as possible, and to keep the turn-around time in port to a minimum, factors that have been the root cause of several major disasters within the last 20 years.

BOILER EXPLOSION ON THE *SULTANA*, 1865

The surrender of Confederate forces in April 1865 marked the end of the American Civil War, leaving thousands of freed Union prisoners stranded in the South. Most were in poor health, and the authorities wanted to get them home as quickly as possible. They were taken to Vicksburg, where they boarded steamers for the journey north along the Mississippi to Cairo, Illinois. The *Sultana*, built in 1863, was one of the many paddle-steamers plying the river between New Orleans and St Louis, carrying passengers, mail and merchandise, that were pressed into service as transports.

She left Vicksburg at 2 am on 26 April, carrying about 85 crew, 70 paying passengers and some 2,300 returning soldiers. (She was licensed to carry only 276 passengers, but given the circumstances, the rules were ignored.) Grossly overloaded, she lumbered upstream, with smoke belching from her tall, twin smoke-stacks and her side-wheels thrashing the water, reaching Memphis 17 hours

later. Her four boilers were of the new tubular type, and the muddy river water meant that the narrow pipes had to be unclogged twice – once at Vicksburg and again at Helena.

At Memphis, she took on more coal, then resumed her journey up river. Eight miles (13 kilometres) out of Memphis, at 2.40 am on 27 April, one of the *Sultana*'s boilers exploded, hurling jagged fragments of red-hot steel through decks covered in sleeping soldiers. Within minutes, two more boilers went up, and a raging fire swept through the stricken steamboat, incinerating passengers in their bunks and collapsing the decks above. Hundreds leapt screaming into the water, only to be crushed as the smoke-stacks came crashing down. On hearing the explosion, other boats rushed to the scene, but could do no more than look on as fire reduced the *Sultana* to a smoking hulk. No accurate records have survived, but it was estimated that around 1,600 people died – more than were lost on the *Titanic*.

COLLISION OF THE *PRINCESS ALICE* AND THE *BYWELL CASTLE*, 1878

Steamer excursions were a popular recreation for the Londoners of Victorian times, and numerous companies offered day trips down the Thames to seaside towns like Gravesend and Sheerness. One such was the London Steamboat Company, and the finest ship in their fleet was the 219-foot (67-metre) *Princess Alice*, a side-wheel paddle-steamer with a top speed of 12 knots (22 kph), elegantly fitted out with a mahogany-panelled saloon, comfortable parlours and a bandstand.

Opposite: *A day trip to the seaside ended in tragedy when the excursion steamer* Princess Alice *collided with the collier* Bywell Castle *on the Thames in 1878.*

heading down river under ballast with the 2-knot (4-kph) ebb tide beneath her. In those days, there were neither traffic separation schemes nor collision regulations to guide a master's decisions, and as the two ships closed each other, Captain Grinstead of the *Princess Alice* suffered an agonizing few moments of indecision. Then he made the fatal error of turning to port, putting his vessel across the bows of the collier, whose speed he had underestimated.

A collision was inevitable. The *Bywell Castle* ploughed into the *Alice*, hitting her on the starboard side, just aft of the paddle-box, and ripping an enormous hole abreast of the engine room. The steamer broke in two and sank within five minutes, while the tide carried the *Bywell Castle* some distance downstream before her captain was able to drop his anchors. Hundreds of passengers who had been on the deck of the *Princess Alice* were thrown into the river, while those below were carried down with the ship. Boats from the *Bywell Castle* and a nearby pleasure steamer, which rushed to assist, found a scene of horror, the water thick with dead and dying passengers. Many were swept down river by the tide, scrabbling hopelessly at the hull of the collier, whose sides were too high to clamber over. An estimated 645 people lost their lives.

FIRE ON THE *GENERAL SLOCUM*, 1904

One of the most tragic events in the history of New York City was the fire that gutted the pleasure steamer *General Slocum* in 1904. The *General* was a typical river steamboat from the turn of the century, with a wooden hull, shallow draft, low freeboard and a couple of promenade decks overlooked by two tall smoke-stacks. She was owned by the Knickerbocker Steamboat Company, and on 15 June 1904 she had been booked to take the younger members of the St Mark's Lutheran Evangelical Church on a Sunday School trip. More than 1,300 mothers and children, mostly from the poor East Side district, gathered at the Third Street landing, chattering excitedly at the prospect of a steamboat cruise.

The *General Slocum* gave a few blasts on her whistle and pulled away from the jetty, heading north up New York's East River. An hour later, as she steamed through Hell Gate Channel, a fire broke

At 6 pm on 3 September 1878, she set out from Gravesend and headed up river towards London. It had been fine and warm, and the *Princess Alice* was crowded with an estimated 700 trippers returning home after an enjoyable day at the seaside. As she steamed along Gallion's Reach, about a mile (1.6 kilometres) short of her destination at North Woolwich Pier, she met the collier *Bywell Castle*

Opposite: *The high sides of the collier, Bywell Castle, prevented many of the passengers rescuing themselves. 645 people lost their lives.*

Left: *Almost 1,000 people, most of them women and children, died when the paddle steamer* General Slocum *caught fire on New York's Hudson River.*

out in a locker amidships where paint and oil were stored. The blaze spread rapidly, fanned by a stiff breeze, and the captain decided to try to ground on Brother Island, half a mile away, as the near-by Harlem shore was lined with oil tanks. Meanwhile, the terrified passengers were forced aft by the flames, where the hand-rails splintered under the weight of the crowd, spilling women and children into the water.

Other vessels rushed to the *General Slocum*'s aid, including a tug that managed to come alongside the starboard paddle-box and take off several dozen people before it too caught fire and had to withdraw. Fire-brigade boats were called out, but found it difficult to approach because there were so many people struggling in the water. The steamer eventually grounded on the island, but by that time it was practically burnt out. During the 30 minutes that the fire had raged, 955 passengers, mostly women and children, and two crew members died of burns or drowning. A further 180 were injured; only 251 escaped unscathed.

An inquiry criticized the owners of the *General Slocum* for having no organized emergency procedures. It also found that her fire hoses were rotten and unserviceable, and her lifebelts were stowed out of reach of the passengers.

THE *DOÑA PAZ* DISASTER, 1987

The Republic of the Philippines is a nation of islands – 7,100 of them – stretching for 1,150 miles (1,850 kilometres) north to south and 700 miles (1,127 kilometres) east to west. The 880 inhabited islands support a population of over 50 million, so it is no surprise that Filipinos rely heavily on ferries as a means of transport: in 1987, passenger manifests recorded that no less than 11 million people travelled on local ferry services. Unfortunately, the country also has a poor safety record – it has been estimated that an incredible 20,000–40,000 people die at sea each year in the Philippines, many in capsizes and 'man overboard' accidents in the thousands of small, overcrowded boats and barges that ply between the smaller islands. But the Filipino merchant fleet also contains about 100 large ferries (over 250 grt/700 cubic metres), one of

which suffered the worst ever peacetime disaster at sea – a disaster that claimed almost three times as many lives as the *Titanic* tragedy.

The *Doña Paz* was a 2,324-ton (2,361-tonne) passenger ferry belonging to Sulpicio Lines, built in 1963 in Japan and measuring 305 feet (93 metres) long with a 45-foot (14-metre) beam. On the morning of Sunday, 20 December 1987, she left Tacloban, on the island of Leyte, bound for the capital, Manila, 375 miles (600 kilometres) to the north, and crowded with passengers who planned to spend the Christmas holidays with relatives. The ship was licensed to carry 1,518 persons, but on this occasion, she was grossly overloaded. The passenger manifest recorded 1,586 people, but the actual number on board was around 4,400 – bodies were crushed four to a bed in the cabins, and hundreds more lay on mats in the corridors and spread across the ferry's three decks.

Night fell dark and moonless as the *Doña Paz* steamed north across the Sibuyan Sea, in the heart of the archipelago, heading for the strait between Mindoro and Marinduque islands – the busiest shipping lane in the Philippines. By 10 pm, there was only one junior officer on the bridge; the others were watching TV and drinking beer in the galley. Meanwhile, the 629-ton (639-tonne) oil tanker *Vector* was steaming in the opposite direction, carrying a cargo of 8,800 barrels of petroleum products. Why the two vessels did not see each other's lights is not known, but soon after 10 pm they collided, immediately setting the tanker's dangerous cargo ablaze. A huge fireball erupted as the leaking petrol spread across the surface of the water, turning both ships into a raging inferno.

Amazingly, the *Doña Paz* had no radio, so no distress signals could be sent. Another ferry spotted the blaze from 8 miles (13 kilometres) away and steamed towards the sinking ships, arriving at about 10.30 pm. Her captain described how he saw 'big flames as high as a ten-storey building' and searched the surrounding waters for three-and-a-half hours. They found only 26 survivors, all suffering from serious burns: 24 from the *Doña Paz*, which finally foundered at around midnight, and two from the *Vector*, which went down a few hours later. The following morning, badly burned bodies began to be washed up on the beaches of Mindoro Island, and for a week afterwards, bloated corpses floated to the surface from the wreck site. But in all, only 275 bodies were recovered.

At first, the authorities claimed that only the 1,586 manifested passengers had been on board, but as more and more distraught relatives came forward to say that members of their families had sailed on the *Doña Paz*, the number increased to a staggering 4,317. Add to this the 58 crew, plus 11 crew from the *Vector*, and the death toll reaches 4,386 – the biggest ever peacetime loss of life at sea.

A board of inquiry found that the Coast Guard had been negligent in allowing the *Doña Paz* to sail in its overcrowded and under-equipped condition: four senior officers were dismissed and 16 others were reassigned. A further marine inquiry laid the blame for the collision on the *Vector*, although the tanker's owners continued to claim that the *Doña Paz* had been responsible.

BOARD OF INQUIRY

The Coast Guard had been negligent in the case of the *Doña Paz* by allowing it to sail overcrowded and under-equipped – four senior officers were dismissed and 16 others were reassigned.

Left: *The Doña Paz disaster in 1987 claimed almost three times as many lives as the Titanic.*

Below: *The* Herald of Free Enterprise *lying on its side in the shallow waters near Zeebrugge.*

THE *HERALD OF FREE ENTERPRISE* DISASTER, 1987

The 'ro-ro' (roll-on, roll-off) ferry is a descendant of the LST (Landing Ship, Tank) of World War 2 – a ship fitted with doors and ramps in the bow, stern or sides that allow vehicles to be loaded and unloaded by simply driving them on and off. In effect, the ship is a floating multi-storey car-park, and the arrangement allows for a rapid (and economical) turn-around in port.

But ever since the early development of commercial 'ro-ro' vessels, there have been fears that their design is inherently unsafe. As long ago as

1953, the British Rail ferry *Princess Victoria* was lost in heavy weather on the Stranraer to Larne crossing. Her stern door was damaged by large waves, and water washing along the car-deck flooded into the hull, causing a severe list. The captain bravely tried to seek shelter, but the ferry finally capsized about 5 miles (8 kilometres) outside Belfast Lough, taking the lives of all but 41 of the 174 people aboard.

The capsize of the 'ro-ro' ferry *Herald of Free Enterprise* off Zeebrugge, with the loss of 193 lives, was the worst British maritime disaster in recent years, and one that brought to public attention the long-standing debate over the seaworthiness of

such vessels. The ship, which was built in 1980 in Bremerhaven, Germany, left Zeebrugge at 7 pm on Friday, 6 March 1987, on a routine cross-channel trip to Dover. On board were 543 passengers, mostly British day-trippers, 80 crew, and a cargo of 84 cars and 42 lorries. As the ferry pulled away from the dock, the bow doors were still open (to save time on turn-around, it was normal practice to close the doors while the ship was heading for the harbour entrance). A recent cut in the number of deck officers meant that responsibility for checking that the bow doors were closed fell to the chief officer, whose duties also required his presence on the bridge as the ship left her berth. He could not be in two places at once, so the door checking was delegated to a seaman on the car-deck, but on this occasion, he was allegedly asleep in his cabin as the ferry left port.

Unaware that the doors were open (they were not visible from the bridge), the captain took the ship up to full speed as she passed the end of Zeebrugge breakwater and entered the open sea. As she pitched into the gentle swell, the open bow dipped beneath the surface and scooped up thousands of tons of sea-water, which roared along the car-deck, sweeping vehicles and crew in its path. The weight of water and displaced cargo caused a list to port, which increased as more and more water flowed in through the open doors, and in less than two minutes, the *Herald of Free Enterprise* lay right over on her beam-ends and sank.

The loss of life would have been even greater if the ship had not settled on a shallow sandbank, in only 30 feet (9 metres) of water, leaving her starboard side above the waves. As it was, the interior of the ship became a nightmare of smashing glass, falling furniture, tumbling bodies and frantic efforts to escape. Rescue services were on the spot within 15 minutes of the capsize and, aided by the cool-headed efficiency of the crew and individual acts of heroism by the passengers, they succeeded in saving more than 400 lives.

A Court of Inquiry following the *Herald of Free Enterprise* disaster recommended that 'ro-ro' ferries should have closed-circuit TV to monitor the car deck; indicator lights on the bridge to show that bow

and stern doors are closed; and a boarding-card system to record accurately passenger numbers. In 1990, the IMO introduced regulations to reduce the risks of car-deck flooding but they applied only to vessels built after 1990.

The provision of indicator lights on the bridge had been suggested by Townsend Thoresen officers several times previously, but had been dismissed by the deputy chief superintendent of the company with the comment, 'Do they need an indicator to tell them whether the deck storekeeper is awake and sober? My goodness!' The Court of Inquiry concluded: 'If this sensible suggestion . . . had received the

Above: *The loss of life on board the* Herald of Free Enterprise *would have been much greater if the ship had not settled on a sandbank in only 30 feet of water.*

Above: The bow visor of the Estonia, which was torn off during heavy weather, is recovered from the sea bed.

serious consideration it deserved, this disaster may well have been prevented.'

THE *ESTONIA* DISASTER, 1994

Captain Richard Cahill, a respected authority on shipping casualties, wrote in 1990 that the tragic fate of the *Herald of Free Enterprise* '. . . only confirmed what knowledgeable seafarers, surveyors, naval architects, shipbuilders and ship owners have known for years. These ships ['ro-ro' vessels] are inherently unseaworthy. It remains to be seen whether economic considerations will again prevail over considerations of safety.' Although the British government swiftly implemented the recommendations of the Court of Inquiry into the *Herald of Free Enterprise*, the fundamental flaw in the design of 'ro-ro' vessels – their inherent instability when the car deck is flooded – was not tackled. And it was this flaw that was realized with horrific finality when the 'ro-ro' ferry *Estonia* capsized and sank in 1994, causing the deaths of 852 people.

The *Estonia* was a 'ro-ro' ferry of 15,598 grt (43,674 cubic metres) built in Germany in 1980 and operated by the Estline Marine Company. She left Tallinn, the capital of Estonia (where she was registered), at 7.15 pm on 27 September 1994 on a scheduled voyage to Stockholm, 225 miles (360 kilometres) away. Seas were moderate as she steamed westwards along the Gulf of Finland at her service speed of 14 knots (26 kph), but as she cleared the Estonian coast, the south-west wind picked up to Force 7 or 8 and the wave height increased to between 10 and 15 feet (3 and 5 metres). The ship began to pitch and roll, and a few passengers became seasick, but the conditions were not out of the ordinary.

Then, at around 1 am, a series of loud bangs was heard from the bow area, and a crew member was sent to investigate, but he found nothing unusual. Further banging noises were heard over the next 10–15 minutes, and at around 1.15 am, the bow visor broke free, ripping open the loading ramp as it fell forward into the sea. Large amounts of water rushed into the car-deck, and within a few minutes the ship had developed a 15-degree list to starboard. In the next ten minutes, the list

increased rapidly to over 40 degrees and the engines stopped. Doors and windows on the starboard side were smashed by the waves, allowing water to rush in, and by 1.35 am, the ferry was lying on its beam-ends.

In the words of the official report into the disaster, 'The ship sank rapidly, stern first, and disappeared from the radar screens of ships in the area at about 0150 hrs.' The *Estonia* had transmitted her first distress call at 1.22 am and sounded the lifeboat alarm, but there was no time for an organized evacuation. Around 300 people managed to reach the decks before the ship capsized, the rest having been trapped below by falling objects and general panic in the narrow stairs and passages. Other ships arrived on the scene within an hour of the ferry sinking, but the first helicopter did not arrive until 3.05 am. Of those who made it on to the decks, about 160 managed to climb into liferafts, and a few others scrambled on to upturned lifeboats. In all, 137 people survived the disaster, and 95 bodies were recovered from the sea. But the wreck of the *Estonia*, lying on her starboard side in 260 feet (79 metres) of water, became the final resting place of 757 men, women and children.

The commission investigating the *Estonia* disaster found that the ferry's bow visor locking devices were not strong enough to cope with the conditions and failed due to wave-induced impacts. She capsized because large amounts of water entered the car-deck, causing loss of stability and subsequent flooding of the accommodation decks. The SOLAS amendments issued in 1990 following the *Herald of Free Enterprise* disaster have now been back-dated to apply to all 'ro-ro' passenger ferries regardless of age, but these still do not deal with the problem of instability once the car-deck is flooded. Regulations of a higher standard (the Stockholm Agreement) were introduced independently by several northern European countries, including the UK, Ireland, Germany, Norway, Sweden and Denmark.

Right: The Estonia's *lifeboats could not be launched because of the severe list that developed within a few minutes of the car deck being flooded.*

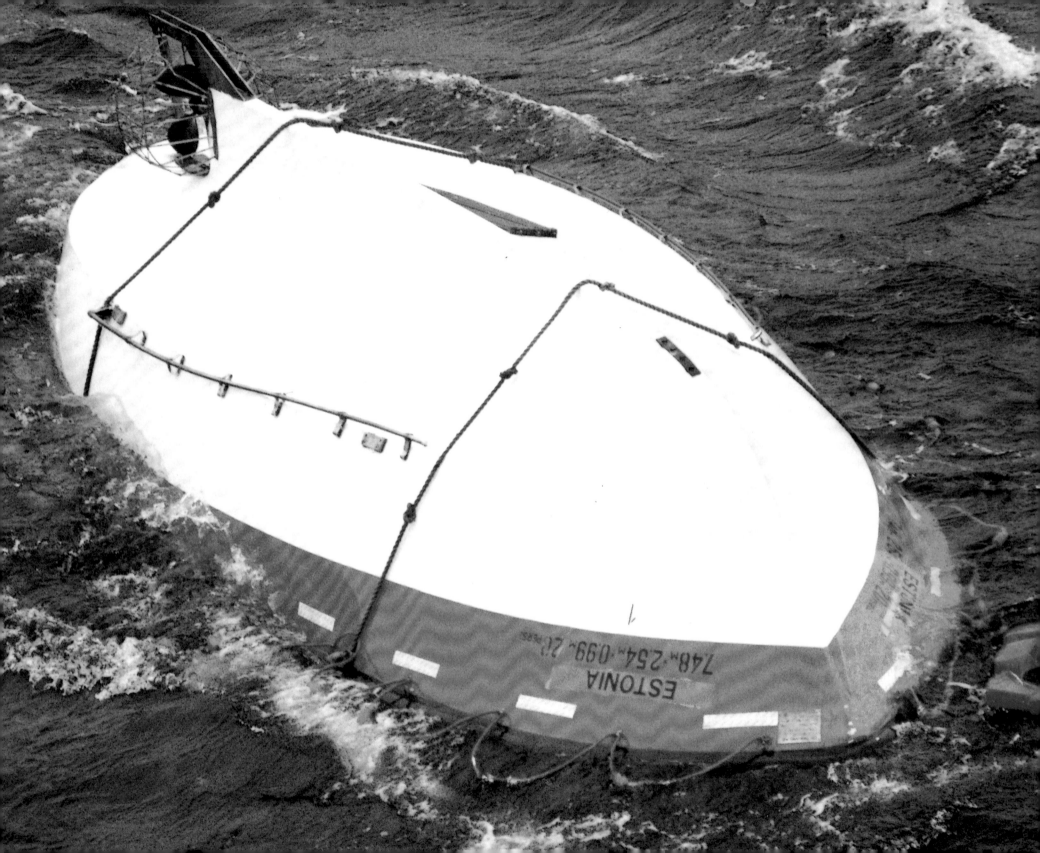

CHAPTER SEVEN

OILTANKERS AND CARGO SHIPS

In the 19th century, marine engineers discovered that big motor vessels were more economical to run than small ones – the transport cost per ton of cargo decreased with increasing size. This important commercial fact was reflected in the trend towards ever larger tankers and bulk carriers in the 20th century.

The deadweight tonnage of the world's biggest tankers increased from 24,000 dwt (24,384 tonnes) in the late 1940s, through 100,000 dwt (101,600 tonnes) in the early 1960s, to the development of Very Large Crude Carriers (VLCCs) of 200,000–400,000 dwt (203,200–406,400 tonnes) in the late 1960s and early 1970s. The biggest ship yet constructed, the ULCC (Ultra Large Crude Carrier) *Jahre Viking* – 564,763 dwt (573,799 tonnes), 1,504 feet long (458 metres) and 226 feet (69 metres) wide, with a draught of 80 feet (24 metres) – was built in Japan in 1979. In addition to the many lives lost in tanker and cargo ship disasters, considerable environmental and economic damage has been caused by oil spills.

EXPLOSION ON THE *MONT BLANC*, 1917

On the morning of 6 December 1917, the French munitions ship *Mont Blanc* arrived in the outer harbour of Halifax, Nova Scotia, carrying 5,000 tons (5,080 tonnes) of high explosives and other chemicals. As she passed through the narrows into Bedford Basin, she met the Norwegian steamship *Imo* travelling in the opposite direction. Although visibility was excellent and the ships had plenty of room to pass, confusion arose about who was going where, and the two vessels collided. Captain Lamodec on the *Mont Blanc*, acutely aware of his dangerous cargo, managed to manoeuvre his vessel so that the *Imo* struck forward of the main hold and its huge load of TNT. But the impact smashed several barrels of benzol that had been lashed on

deck, and the fuel found its way below, igniting a cargo of explosive picric acid stowed in the forward hold.

A raging fire erupted, which the crew foolishly tried to contain until it was too late to scuttle the ship. As they took to the boats and rowed frantically for the shore, the main cargo went up in the biggest man-made explosion the world had ever known (it wasn't exceeded until the first nuclear bomb was detonated). An incredibly powerful shock wave ripped across the harbour and the town, destroying ships, flattening buildings and tossing railway wagons around like toys. An estimated 2,000 people died, including all 200 pupils in Dartmouth School and every woman and child in the local orphans' home. Another 8,000 people were injured, and 3,000 houses were destroyed.

THE WRECK OF THE *TORREY CANYON*, 1967

When the Torrey Canyon was stranded on the Seven Stones reef, 13 miles (21 kilometres) west of Land's End, England, it was the first time that the world had had to deal with a major oil spill. The tanker's entire cargo – almost 120,000 tons (121,920 tonnes) of crude oil – escaped into the sea, causing severe pollution on the shores of Cornwall, the Channel Islands and Brittany. It was an accident that should never have happened, a perfect example of what accident investigators call an 'incident pit' – a series of small events, each seemingly unimportant, but each deepening a hole from which, eventually, the victim cannot escape.

Opposite: Attempts to control the oil pollution from the Torrey Canyon by bombing the ship and burning its cargo merely broke the hull in two. The oil refused to burn.

Above: The Torrey Canyon, grounded on the Seven Stones rocks, provided the world's first experience of a major marine oil spill.

Captain Pastrengo Rugiati, the master of the *Torrey Canyon*, was proud of his ship. Built in 1959 in Newport News, Virginia, she had been extended in 1964 in Japan to give her a length of 974 feet (297 metres) and a deadweight tonnage of 118,285 (331,200 cubic metres). At the time, this made her the 13th largest vessel in the world. She departed Mena al Ahmadi in the Persian Gulf on 18 February 1967, bound for the Welsh refinery port of Milford Haven with a cargo of 119,190 tons (121,100 tonnes) of Kuwaiti crude. She had a fast and uneventful voyage around the Cape of Good Hope, and by dawn on Saturday, 18 March, she was about 40 miles (64 kilometres) south-south-west of the Scilly Isles, steaming on autopilot at about 16 knots (30 kph). Cloudy weather had prevented the taking of astronomical sights since noon on Friday, and the Loran position-fixing equipment was not working, so navigation had been by dead-reckoning for the previous 18 hours.

The planned course was the normal route for large ships approaching from the south: to pass west of the Scilly Islands, then turn right, heading north-east into the Bristol Channel. Thus, when the first officer picked up the Scillies on radar at about 6.30 am, he was surprised to see them off his port bow rather than to starboard, as expected; obviously, wind and current had set the ship to the east of her intended course. The officer turned the tanker to port until she was headed towards the Bishop Rock, west of the Scillies, then woke the captain and told him what he had done.

Captain Rugiati was angry that the ship's course had been altered without his permission. 'With our original heading of 018 degrees, would we clear the Scillies?' he asked. 'Yes,' was the reply. 'Then continue on 018. I intend to pass east of the Scillies.' Later, the captain would claim that his reason for taking the eastern route was to save time, as he had to catch high water at Milford Haven on Saturday evening, but going to the west would have taken only half an hour longer. It is possible that he had been irritated by his first mate's independent action, reacted impulsively and then was too proud to back down.

There are two deep-water channels between the Scilly Isles and Land's End, separated by the dangerous rocks of the Seven Stones reef. One, over 11 miles (18 kilometres) wide, lies between the Seven Stones Lightship and the Longships Lighthouse off Land's End; the other, about 6 miles (10 kilometres) wide, lies between the Seven Stones and the Scillies. At 8 am, with the captain, third officer and helmsman on the bridge, the *Torrey Canyon* was 4 miles (6 kilometres) south-east of St Mary's, still heading 018 degrees at 16 knots. During the next 40 minutes, as the huge tanker drew ever closer to the Seven Stones reef, the captain decided to turn left through the narrower western channel, and altered the ship's course to due north before re-engaging the autopilot. Suddenly, he found himself within a few miles of rocks and islands, with two fishing boats ahead and fishing floats in the water around the ship. The *Torrey Canyon* was headed directly towards the Seven Stones, and still travelling at full speed, but even at this point Captain Rugiati could have avoided disaster by turning right into deep water. Unfortunately, he seems to have been intent on a left turn.

He rushed on to the bridge, shouting at the helmsman to turn hard to port. The helmsman put the wheel over, but to his amazement, nothing happened. 'She's not turning!' he yelled. The captain's first thought was that the steering gear was malfunctioning, and he began to call the engineer, then to his horror he noticed that the autopilot lever was in a position that left the steering wheel disengaged. He ran over, set the lever to manual and spun the wheel to port. The gyro-compass clicked off the degrees as the bow slowly turned to the left, but it was too late. With a slow, thunderous grinding, the *Torrey Canyon* ripped her hull open on the Seven Stones reef.

The aftermath of the wreck is now history. Salvage attempts were made, during which one of the salvage crew was killed by an explosion. Then, when the ship began to break up, the British Government tried to burn the oil by bombing the wreck from the air. But their attempts failed, allowing the huge oil slick to pollute beaches and kill seabirds and marine life along hundreds of miles of coast in Cornwall, Brittany and the Channel Islands.

A Liberian Government Board of Inquiry found that the wreck of the *Torrey Canyon* had been caused by human error, and that Captain Rugiati was responsible. He had been imprudent in deciding to pass east of the Scilly Isles and was found to be negligent on five counts: deciding to use the channel to the west of the Seven Stones; failing to turn right at 8.40 am; leaving the ship on autopilot while navigating close to land; not reducing his speed; and not having instituted a standard practice for the operation of the autopilot controls. Captain Rugiati lost his master's licence and retired a sick, broken man.

NEGLIGENCE

Captain Rugiati was found to be negligent on five counts: deciding to use the channel west of the Seven Stones; failing to turn right at 8.40 am; leaving the ship on autopilot while navigating close to land; not reducing his speed; and not having instituted a standard practice for the operation of autopilot controls.

Left: *The* Torrey Canyon *breaks up in the aftermath of one of the biggest ecological disasters to hit the channel.*

THE LOSS OF THE *BERGE ISTRA*, 1975

The *Berge Istra* was one of four ships built in 1972 for the General Ore International Corporation. These huge vessels were over 1,000 feet (305 metres) in length and 220,000 dwt (616,000 cubic metres), being designed to carry both oil and dry bulk cargoes. The *Berge Istra* operated on a circular route, loading oil in the Persian Gulf and taking it to northern Europe, then sailing in ballast to Brazil, where she picked up iron ore for Japan, then back to the Gulf in ballast to start the circuit again.

On her final voyage, she had taken a cargo of crude from the Iranian oil terminal at Kharg Island to Rotterdam, and cleaned her tanks as she crossed the Atlantic to Brazil. There, at the port of Tubarao, she took on 185,244 tons (188,208 tonnes) of iron ore. She sailed at around 3 pm on 28 November 1975, bound for Kimitsu, Japan, via the Cape of Good Hope and the Sunda Strait, with 32 officers and crew. On Monday, 29 December, her captain sent a radio message to her owners, giving an ETA at Kimitsu of 8 am on 5 January 1976. But the *Berge Istra* never arrived in Japan, and she was never heard from again.

Her owners showed no undue concern at the lack of further progress reports until their ship failed to arrive at Kimitsu on 5 January. When she did not respond to repeated radio calls, an extensive air and sea search was initiated, involving Japanese, Far Eastern and Australian rescue services, and the American and Philippine air forces. However, they were hampered by the fact that the *Berge Istra's* last known position could only be guessed at by working backwards from the ETA she had given. There had been no bad weather, and she could have disappeared anywhere between Japan and the southern Philippines.

The search turned up nothing and was called off on 13 January. But a few days later, a Japanese fishing boat, about 250 miles (400 kilometres) south of the Palau Islands, picked up a liferaft with two Spanish sailors inside. Able Seaman Imeldo Leon told how he had been one of four men working on the fore-deck of the *Berge Istra* on 30 December, when the ship was rocked by two huge explosions aft and began to list to port. As the men scrambled to launch a liferaft, a third, even bigger, explosion ripped through the stern and superstructure, throwing them into the sea. The ship sank quickly, sucking Leon down, but he struggled to the surface and climbed into the raft, pulling one of the others with him. There was no sign of any other survivors. The two men had drifted for 19 days and lived on fish and rainwater after the raft's supplies had run out.

The Board of Investigation into the loss of the *Berge Istra* found that the first explosion was probably the result of inflammable gases, which had collected in the ship's double bottom, being ignited by welding work. This set off further explosions in the pump room and the port fuel tank. Unfortunately, lessons were not learnt. In 1979, the *Berge Vanga*, a sister ship, disappeared in the South Atlantic with 40 crew on board. This time there were no survivors.

THE STRANDING OF THE *AMOCO CADIZ*, 1978

The decade following the *Torrey Canyon* saw more than 50 oil spills of over 5,000 tons (5,080 tonnes) pollute the world's oceans, most of them concentrated in the busy coastal waters on each side of the North Atlantic. But all would be dwarfed by the disaster that struck the Brittany coast in 1978.

The *Amoco Cadiz* sailed from the Persian Gulf in the middle of February 1978, carrying 223,000 tons (226,570 tonnes) of Iranian crude for the refineries of Rotterdam; at 228,500 dwt (639,800 cubic metres), she had almost twice the cargo capacity of the *Torrey Canyon*. She followed the standard route for ships too big to use the Suez Canal: around the Cape of Good Hope, up through the Canary Islands, and across the Bay of Biscay. As the sun rose on 16 March, she entered the traffic separation scheme off Ushant, on the western tip of Brittany, rolling heavily and taking seas on deck in the Force 7 westerly wind. She altered course to starboard to begin heading up the English Channel, then at 9.45 am the ship's steering gear failed.

Opposite: A steering gear failure put the tanker Amoco Cadiz *aground off Brittany in 1978. More than 200,000 tons of crude oil polluted the coast of north-west France.*

Above: Soon after grounding on the Portsall rocks, the Amoco Cadiz *began to break up.*

Captain Bardari stopped the engines and hoisted two black balls at the yard-arm (a signal meaning 'the ship is not under command'), then broadcast a warning to other vessels on the VHF that he had lost his steering. Although he was now drifting in a gale, in a fully loaded VLCC, with a lee shore only 15 miles (24 kilometres) away, he was not unduly alarmed: steering failures were not that rare and usually could be remedied by changing a fuse or switching to a back-up hydraulic system. The problem proved to be a broken hydraulic pipe, and

the engineers struggled to make repairs for more than an hour until another pipe fractured – now the steering could not be restored. At about 11.20 am, Captain Bardari radioed for a tug.

By the time the German tug *Pacific* arrived, at 12.20 pm, the wind had risen to a full gale and had veered to the north-west, while the huge tanker had drifted closer to the rocky coast of Brittany. A hawser was passed to the stricken vessel, and the tug tried to pull her head into the wind, which would allow the tanker's engines to be used to drive her

Left: The bridge and bow are visible in this picture of the Amoco Cadiz *some days after she ran aground.*

away from the coast. But the tug was not powerful enough, and although it managed to check the tanker's drift for a while, the towing line parted at 4.15 pm. Captain Bardari tried to hold his ship off the coast, now only 9 miles (14 kilometres) away, by putting his engines astern, but the single screw was hampered by the uselessly flogging rudder, and wind and tide continued to push the *Amoco Cadiz* towards danger. A more powerful tug was on its way, but it would not arrive until midnight. At 7 pm, the *Pacific* attempted to pass a second cable to the tanker's stern, but to no avail. At 8 pm, with his ship less than 2 miles (3 kilometres) from the rocks, Captain Bardari dropped the port anchor, but still the ship continued to drift. Finally, at 9.04 pm, the *Amoco Cadiz* grounded on the rocks off Portsall, about 15 miles (24 kilometres) north-east of Ushant.

The crew was lifted off by helicopter, and that night the *Amoco Cadiz* began to break up. Over the next few weeks, 223,000 tons (226,570 tonnes) of crude oil escaped from her tanks, polluting the seas and shorelines of north-western France.

The Liberian Government Inquiry into the *Amoco Cadiz* found that, although the ship appeared to comply with the SOLAS regulations, 'events . . . proved all too clearly that she did not in fact have an effective auxiliary steering gear'. Captain Bardari was also criticized for his delay in calling for a tug.

THE COLLISION BETWEEN *ATLANTIC EMPRESS* AND *AEGEAN CAPTAIN*, 1979

Two world records were broken when two VLCCs, the *Atlantic Empress* and the *Aegean Captain*, collided off Tobago in the Caribbean Sea on 19 July 1979 – the biggest-ever oil spill from a tanker, and the biggest-ever vessel to become a total loss.

The Liberian-registered *Aegean Captain* had taken on 200,500 tons (203,700 tonnes) of crude at Curaçao and Bonaire, and was bound for Singapore. On the evening of 19 July, she rounded the north end of Tobago and, at 7 pm, as she laid a course for the Cape of Good Hope, she entered a squall of very heavy rain. Meanwhile, the Greek-registered *Atlantic Empress* was approaching Tobago from the opposite direction, having sailed around the Cape from the Persian Gulf with a 270,000-ton (274,320-tonne) cargo. As fate would have it, the two supertankers met in the middle

Above: Surface booms partially contain the slick while a smaller tanker offloads oil from the stranded Exxon Valdez.

Opposite: Only 35,000 tons of crude escaped from the Exxon Valdez, but it caused widespread damage to the delicate Alaskan environment.

of the squall, neither having spotted the other in the dark and the rain until they were only a mile apart. By that time, collision was unavoidable.

When the *Aegean Captain* struck the *Atlantic Empress* on her port side, oil gushed from the ruptured tanks and set both ships ablaze. The *Captain* was abandoned in good order with the loss of only one man, but there was panic on the *Empress*, where the fire was much worse and the crew poorly trained – 29 of the 42 people aboard died. As the two vessels burned, a 25-square-mile (65-square-kilometre) oil slick spread across the sea and threatened the beaches of Tobago. The fire on the *Aegean Captain* was put out and she was towed back to Curaçao to be unloaded, leaking oil as she went. The still-burning *Atlantic Empress* was towed further out to sea until, on 29 July, an explosion ripped her apart amidships. A huge fire erupted, which blazed for several days, smoke and flames billowing 600 feet (180 metres) into the air, until the tanker finally sank on 2 August. In all, an estimated 300,000 tons (304,800 tonnes) of crude oil escaped into the ocean.

Captain Paschalis Chatzipetros of the *Atlantic Empress* refused to attend the Board of Investigation, and his master's licence was revoked. The Board found him negligent in allowing the ship's radio operator, who not only had no watch-keeping certificate, but also was a drunk who suffered from poor eyesight, to stand watch on the bridge of a supertanker at dusk as it entered a rain squall.

THE GROUNDING OF THE *EXXON VALDEZ*, 1989

Although the amount of oil spilled when the *Exxon Valdez* ran aground in Prince William Sound in 1989 was small compared to the *Torrey Canyon* and *Amoco Cadiz* disasters, it was the worst spill in US history and caused enormous public outrage. Newspapers and television screens were filled with potent images of the pristine Alaskan wilderness fouled by 35,000 tons (35,560 tonnes) of sticky brown crude. For years, environmentalists had warned of the dangers of taking VLCCs through the tricky channels of Prince William Sound, but it gave them no satisfaction to see their predictions come true.

Oil and gas were discovered on the North Slope of Alaska in 1968, but its extraction and transportation posed many problems. The solution finally decided on was the Trans-Alaska Pipeline, which stretches for 800 miles (1,300 kilometres) from Prudhoe Bay on the Arctic coast to the ice-free port of Valdez in the south. This went into operation in 1977. The 211,469-dwt (592,113-cubic-metre) *Exxon Valdez* left the loading terminal at Valdez at 9 pm on 24 March 1989, under the command of Captain Joseph Hazelwood. For the first 20 miles (32 kilometres) she was conned by a pilot, then the captain gave the helm to his third officer, Gregory Cousins, in whom he had great confidence. He told Cousins to take the ship south to clear some ice, then turn right to pass between the ice and the rocks of Bligh reef, a few miles further off to the south. Then Hazelwood left the bridge to attend to some paperwork. It was 11.45 pm.

For some reason, the third officer did not initiate his turn until the ship was more than a mile (1.6 kilometres) past the point where the captain had said he should begin turning. With mounting anxiety, Cousins watched the ship's head swing around with agonizing slowness, realizing that he had left it too late. He called Captain Hazelwood and said, 'I think we are in serious trouble.' Before the captain could get to the bridge, a series of sickening thuds told him that the *Exxon Valdez* had grounded on the Bligh Reef.

No one was hurt, and later the ship was refloated and towed away for repairs, but the oil spill contaminated some 1,100 miles (1,770 kilometres) of Alaskan coastline, killing many thousands of birds and animals. In addition to the environmental damage, the local economy was also severely affected. The clean-up operation and compensation claims cost the oil company Exxon more than a billion dollars.

Captain Hazelwood was indicted on a charge of criminal mischief, but later was acquitted. It was claimed that he had been drinking on the night of the accident, but it is doubtful that this contributed to events. More serious was his poor judgement in leaving a competent, but relatively inexperienced, officer alone on the bridge in a difficult pilotage situation.

CHAPTER EIGHT

WHALERS, FISHING BOATS, LIFEBOATS & YACHTS

Those who earn their living from the sea have always been closest to its dangers, and not a year goes by without the sea claiming its toll of fishermen's lives – in the UK alone, 26 fishing boats were lost in 1996, and 21 in 1997. In the 19th century, when the fishing fleet was far larger and boats carried little if anything in the way of safety equipment, the casualty rate was much higher.

The whalers also had a hard life, their voyages keeping them at sea for up to three years at a time, and the hunt often taking them into remote and dangerous waters. The lifeboat services, which were established in Europe and North America in the 19th century, were largely manned by fishermen, and with the decline of the coasting trade, fishing boats, yachts and motor boats now account for a large proportion of call-outs.

THE WRECK OF THE WHALE SHIP ESSEX, 1820

One of the most remarkable stories in the history of seafaring is the tale of the Nantucket whaler *Essex*, as recorded by her first mate, Owen Chase. The *Essex* departed Nantucket on 12 August 1819 for a two-and-a-half-year voyage to the Pacific whaling grounds, with a crew of 21 under Captain George Pollard. She rounded the Horn in December and made her way north along the South American coast, then headed west into the hunting grounds that lay along the equator.

On 20 November 1820, some 1,300 miles (2,100 kilometres) west of the Galápagos Islands, the *Essex* was attacked while the ship's boats were out on the hunt. Owen Chase had returned to the *Essex* to repair his boat, which had been holed by a blow from a whale's fluke, when he saw a large sperm whale swim towards the *Essex* and ram her. 'The ship brought up as suddenly and violently as if she had struck a rock, and trembled for a few seconds,' he wrote. Then she began to settle by the head.

Chase ordered men to the pumps and recalled the other whale boats, noticing the rogue whale thrashing, 'apparently in convulsions, on top of the water' and snapping its jaws. It then turned and rammed the ship a second time. Within ten minutes, the *Essex* lay over on her beam-ends, and the 21 men found themselves facing the prospect of being cast adrift in three open whale boats, over 1,000 miles (1,600 kilometres) from the nearest land.

The crippled ship remained afloat for another day, during which the sailors retrieved navigation equipment, 600 pounds (272 kilograms) of hard bread and 65 gallons (295 litres) of water per boat. They were also able to fashion sailing rigs from the ship's spars and canvas. The nearest land was the Marquesas Islands, 1,000 miles (1,600 kilometres) to the south-west, but they were afraid of dangerous savages and decided their best chance was to head south to latitude 25 degrees, where they would pick up westerly winds that should take them to Chile. At midday on 22 November, they cast off from the disintegrating wreck of the *Essex* and headed south.

The three little boats endured gales, leaks, burning sun and constant soakings, and on 20 December arrived at a tiny, uninhabited island, where the men stayed for a week, eating fish, crabs, seabirds and eggs. But there was little hope of being rescued from this remote spot, so on 27 December they set off again, leaving behind three men who preferred to take their chances on the island. The three boats headed east towards South America, but soon became separated in bad weather.

An incredible ordeal followed, during which the men suffered thirst and hunger, sunburn, salt-water

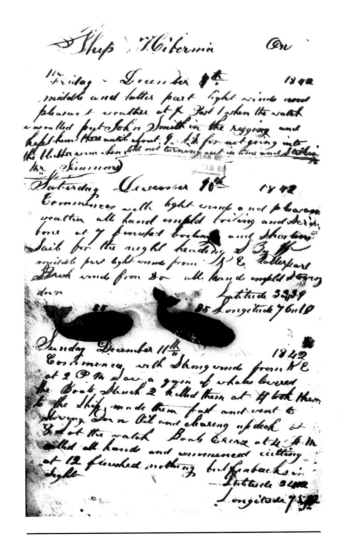

Above: *A 19th-century log book, detailing three days in a voyage that could involve three years and much danger (opposite).*

Above: Commercial whaling has largely died out, although Norway and Japan continue to hunt whales. These vessels were the last whale ships to operate from Australia.

Below: This picture of a fishing boat wrecked off Trouville in northern France illustrates the hazards faced regularly by fishermen in the 19th century.

sores, head winds and bad weather. There were five men in Chase's boat, and when the first one died, his colleagues wrapped him up in his shirt and buried him at sea. But when a second man died, Chase broached the subject of keeping the body for food, as they had provisions enough for only three more days. 'I have no language to paint the anguish of our souls in this dreadful dilemma,' he later wrote, but the others agreed and butchered their friend's corpse, eating the heart and liver and hanging strips of flesh to dry in the sun. About eight days later, on 17 February 1821, they sighted an island (one of the Juan Fernandez group), and on the following day they were picked up by an English brig.

Of the five men who left the island in Chase's boat, three survived. The captain's boat was picked up further south, with two survivors: they too had resorted to cannibalism, with the added horror of drawing lots to decide who would die and who would do the killing. They had been at sea in open boats for over 90 days and sailed over 3,000 miles (4,800 kilometres). The third boat was never found, but the three men on the desert island were picked up two months later.

Owen Chase's written account of the whale's attack on the Essex was later a source of inspiration for Herman Melville's famous novel, *Moby Dick*.

FISHING BOAT DISASTERS

In the days of sail, before dependable weather forecasts, many thousands of small fishing boats were lost when they were caught out by bad weather; one or two big storms could wipe out an entire fishing fleet. Two storms, in 1832 and 1881, claimed a total of 27 boats and 163 men from Shetland, while a single south-easterly gale, in August 1848, wiped out 124 boats and 100 men from the Scottish ports of Wick and Peterhead. The worst of all was the great Eyemouth Disaster of October 1881, when a storm took the lives of 191 fishermen, leaving behind 107 widows and 351 fatherless children in the tiny fishing communities of south-east Scotland.

After World War 2, powerful diesel engines, radios and regular weather forecasts promised to make the fisherman's lot a little safer but, until the advent of satellite images, predicting the weather on Europe's western seaboard was more of an art than a science. The weather systems came from the west, and there were only a few weather ships to provide observations of what was happening in the Atlantic; often, the first indications of severe weather for a fishing boat were a rapidly falling barometer and a wall of dark cloud on the horizon.

That is what happened to six diesel trawlers from Brittany in November 1954. The *Pierre Nelly*, the *Perle d'Arvor*, the *Tendre Berceuse*, the *Tourville*, the *Berceau de Morse* and the *Alain Yvon* were fishing over the banks in the western approaches to the English Channel when they were caught in a hurricane and disappeared without trace. There were no distress signals, no wreckage was seen, and no survivors were found – 70 fishermen from the little ports of Concarneau and Douarnenez were lost. All that was ever found was an empty boat belonging to the *Pierre Nelly*, which drifted ashore on a lonely beach in the Scillies some time after the storm.

In the aftermath of the Brittany disaster, an inquiry recommended that an improved meteorological service be established; that better use be made of radio, and in particular that boats should report their positions regularly; that fishing boats should carry inflatable liferafts; and that large fisheries vessels be permanently on station to provide assistance when necessary.

The English fishing port of Hull is no stranger to the cruelty of the sea – 900 of its boats have been lost in the last 150 years. But the disappearance of the Hull-registered trawler *Gaul*, in 1974, has recently returned to the attention of the public. The *Gaul* was a new boat, built in 1972, a 200-foot (61-metre) 'super-trawler' designed to take the worst conditions that the Arctic fishing grounds could throw at her. She carried all the latest safety equipment, high-quality radio and radar, and enough automatically inflating liferafts to hold 50 people. And she had a highly experienced skipper and crew.

But on, or soon after, 8 February 1974, during a storm on the Harbaken fishing grounds, 70 miles (113 kilometres) north of Norway's North Cape, the

Gaul and her crew of 36 disappeared. After an intensive air and sea search, she was posted missing at Lloyd's; three months later, a Norwegian fishing boat picked up one of her lifebelts, but nothing else was ever found. However, there were persistent rumours that Hull trawlers had been involved in espionage work for British Intelligence, spying on Soviet ships in Arctic waters, and that this might somehow be connected with the *Gaul*'s disappearance.

In 1997, the TV documentary programme *Dispatches*, on the UK's Channel 4, revealed that it had chartered a survey boat with remotely controlled underwater cameras, and within two days of searching had discovered the wreck of the *Gaul*, lying in 900 feet (270 metres) of water close to its last known position. Their pictures showed that the boat did not appear to have suffered any major damage, but offered no other clues as to why she might have foundered. To date, the British Government has declined to reopen the accident investigation.

But undoubtedly some fishing boat disasters have been caused by military activity. One such was the loss of the trawler *Antares*, from Carradale in Argyll, which was dragged beneath the surface when her trawl was snagged by the British nuclear submarine *HMS Trenchant* in November 1990: all four men aboard the fishing boat were drowned. As a result of this tragedy, a system was set up to inform fishermen of areas where submarine exercises might be taking place.

One of the most recent casualties in the long list of fishing boats lost at sea is the *Sapphire*, which foundered on 1 October 1997, only 12 miles (19 kilometres) outside her home port of Peterhead, in north-east Scotland. She went down in heavy seas during a gale, drowning four men from her crew of five. In a break with a long-standing tradition that declares the sea to be a noble resting place, the relatives of the lost fishermen campaigned to have the bodies of their loved ones recovered from the wreck. But the British Government refused any financial assistance and, in a remarkable feat of fund-raising, the campaigners collected the substantial sum of £385,000 quoted by the salvage company in the space of only a week. Despite delays

caused by bad weather, the *Sapphire* was successfully lifted and the lost men were buried on land; then the tragic vessel was towed back to sea and consigned to the deep.

Above: *Despite improvements in boat design and safety equipment, hundreds of fishing boats continue to be lost each year.*

LIFEBOAT DISASTERS

The winter of 1788–89 was a bad one for shipwrecks on the east coast of England. It culminated in the wreck of the sailing ship *Adventure* off South Shields, at the mouth of the River Tyne, on 15 March 1789. Thousands of local people watched helplessly from the shore as the stranded ship was broken apart by the fury of the waves, unable to prevent the loss of all who were on board.

The tragedy prompted a group of local men to establish a rescue boat at the mouth of the Tyne. They sponsored a competition for a suitable design, and the *Original* – an oar-driven boat with built-in cork buoyancy and a self-righting capability – was launched in January 1790. Although the Chinese can lay claim to the first organized rescue service (rescue boats were stationed on the Yangtse River in the mid-18th century), this was the world's first purpose-built lifeboat. Its success led Sir William Hillary to found the National Institution for the Preservation of Life from Shipwreck, which later became the Royal National Lifeboat Institution.

The men and women of Britain's RNLI are, and have always been, volunteers who willingly risk their own lives to save others. Modern lifeboats are state-of-the-art vessels, designed to be self-righting and unsinkable, and they are helmed by some of the world's most experienced and competent seamen,

Opposite: The Tynemouth lifeboat (shown above approaching a shipwreck beneath Tynemouth priory) was the first purpose-built lifeboat to be stationed in the United Kingdom.

Below: Streathead's Original, the first purpose-built lifeboat with buoyancy and self-righting ability, was built at Newcastle in 1789 and served at Tynemouth for 40 years.

Above: 24 yachts were abandoned during the Fastnet disaster, but only five sank. Several, inlcuding the Ariadne *(above) were dismasted.*

but such perilous work has inevitably taken its toll of lives. One of the worst disasters in the history of the RNLI took place in April 1947, when the Mumbles lifeboat in South Wales was called out to assist the 7,000-ton (7,112-tonne) cargo ship *Samtampa*, which was in trouble in heavy weather in Swansea Bay. By the time the lifeboat arrived, the ship had been driven on to the rocks on the east side of the bay and broken into three parts. All 41 of the *Samtampa*'s crew were drowned, and in the morning the Mumbles lifeboat was found bottom-up on the rocks – all eight lifeboatmen had perished too.

THE FASTNET YACHT RACE DISASTER, 1979

The sea is still one of the last preserves of individual freedom and, in Britain at least, it is possible for anyone to buy a yacht or motor boat and take her to sea without being legally required to possess any kind of qualification or certificate of competence. Fortunately, the vast majority of amateur sailors exercise this freedom with responsibility, taking courses in boat-handling, seamanship and navigation before venturing offshore.

However, the world's worst yachting disaster did not involve rash beginners, but happened when a fleet of experienced ocean racing yachtsmen was caught out by a storm of unexpected severity. The Fastnet Race was first held in 1925, being sailed annually until 1931 and every second year thereafter. The challenging course, over 600 miles (970 kilometres) in length, runs from the starting point at Cowes on the Isle of Wight, around the Scilly Isles, then north to the remote Fastnet Rock off the Irish coast, before returning to the finish at Plymouth. When 303 competing yachts crossed the starting line on 11 August 1979, only one life had been lost in the entire history of the race. But as the fleet spread out across the Celtic Sea three days later, it was overtaken by a storm that generated winds of up to Force 11 and enormous, confused seas over 40 feet (12 metres) high. Dozens of yachts were in distress, and a huge rescue operation was mounted, involving 13 lifeboats from both sides of the Irish Sea and several other vessels that were in the area. In the end, 15 lives were lost and 24 yachts were abandoned, five of which foundered.

The inquiry that followed the Fastnet disaster recommended, among other things: further study of the hull design and stability of racing yachts; new requirements for secure watertight hatches; and greater use of VHF radios (only 65 per cent of the competing yachts were equipped with radios).

Left: A yachtsman is winched from the sea during the Fastnet Race disaster of 1979, when a Force 11 storm claimed 15 lives.

CHAPTER NINE

MYSTERIES

The very nature of disaster at sea – often far from shore, with no visible wreckage and no survivors to tell the tale – means that the causes of many tragedies will remain forever unknown.

The history of seafaring is liberally spiced with tales of mystery and intrigue, from the classic case of the *Mary Celeste* to the unusual story of the steamship *Marlborough*, whose mouldy and weed-shrouded hulk was found drifting off Tierra del Fuego in 1913, having disappeared 23 years previously. On board were the scattered bones of her crew, but what fate befell them, whether disease or food poisoning, no one could tell.

THE WRECK OF THE *MOHEGAN*, 1898

The little Cornish church of St Keverne sits on a hilltop above Falmouth Bay, its tower a landmark for passing yachts, its churchyard the last resting place of farmers, fishermen and the victims of shipwreck. To the east of the church, less than a mile (1.6 kilometres) offshore, jagged fangs of black rock pierce the waves, known as *maen eglos* (Church Rocks) in the Cornish tongue. The Manacles, to use their anglicized name, have been the cause of more than 100 shipwrecks, from the *Star Cross* in 1787 to the *Forde* in 1919, and have taken over 1,000 lives. But the most mysterious of these disasters, and the one that claimed the most lives, was the wreck of the steamship *Mohegan*.

The *Mohegan* was a new luxury liner of 6,889 grt (19,289 cubic metres) belonging to the Atlantic Transport Company. On 13 October 1898, she departed Tilbury in London, bound for New York with only 53 passengers, 97 crew and seven cattlemen to tend a cargo of live cattle on deck. She turned south from the Thames and steamed through the English Channel, and by the afternoon of the

14th she had passed Prawle Point and was seen by observers off Plymouth. Dusk merged into a dark and moonless night, but the weather was good and the sea was calm. Nevertheless, at some point a terrible mistake was made – instead of following a course of 260 degrees, which would have taken her clear to the south of the Lizard, the *Mohegan* was heading straight towards the Manacles and the unlit coast behind.

At around 6.45 pm, people at Porthoustock, the fishing village beneath St Keverne, saw the liner's lights and realized that she was steaming towards disaster. The coastguard lookout on the cliff-top fired off a warning rocket, but to no effect – the *Mohegan* ran on to the Manacles at 13 knots (24 kph), striking with such force that the boiler room began to fill immediately; within a few minutes, the generators were flooded and all her lights went out. A distress rocket went up from the ship, but the Porthoustock lifeboat was already being launched, soon to be followed by others from Cadgwith, Falmouth and Polperro. Meanwhile, the liner was rolling in the light swell, making it difficult to lower the boats, while the total darkness and lack of lights made it difficult for the lifeboats to find the stricken ship. Fifteen minutes after striking the rocks, she lay over on her port side and went down by the head, leaving only her masts and funnel showing above the waves. Two boats had got clear, and a few survivors clambered into the rigging, but only 43 lives were saved in all.

The death toll of 106 included the captain and all his officers, so what went wrong will never be known; it can only be assumed that the captain had ordered the wrong course, or that the helmsman

Opposite: An engraving of the US brig Mary Celeste, *probably the most famous of maritime mysteries. It is thought she was abandoned because her crew feared an explosion in her cargo of alcohol.*

had steered the wrong course. The little church at St Keverne served as a makeshift mortuary while local people performed the grisly task of gathering the corpses from the shore (the captain's body was found three months later, washed up headless in Caernarvon Bay, 250 miles/400 kilometres away). Several mass graves were dug in the churchyard, including one beneath the north wall in which no less than 40 coffins were buried.

THE DISAPPEARANCE OF THE *WARATAH*, 1909

When the steamship *Waratah* failed to arrive at Cape Town, South Africa, on 29 July 1909, having sailed from Durban only three days previously, no one believed that this fine, modern vessel could have foundered. Yes, there had been bad weather, but other ships had followed the same route and had suffered no problems, other than anxiety and discomfort. No wreckage had been seen, no bodies were found, no lifeboats were washed ashore – nothing. Marine radio was in its early days, and the *Waratah* did not have a wireless set, so she would have been unable to call for assistance. Surely she must have suffered engine failure and was drifting helplessly, waiting for rescue.

The *Waratah*, built on the Clyde in 1908, was a 465-foot (142-metre) passenger and cargo steamer belonging to the famous Blue Anchor Line. She had called at South Africa on the homeward leg of her second round trip from London to Australia, and when she left Durban on 26 July, she was carrying 92 passengers and 10,000 tons (10,160 tonnes) of general cargo. Her captain thought her a fine ship, although perhaps a little tender, and with a tendency to 'roll and stick'. The coast between Durban and Cape Town was well-known to seafarers for its wild, unpredictable weather and dangerous seas – when a south-westerly gale tore into the 5-knot (9-kph) Agulhas Current, waves 60 feet (18 metres) high were commonplace – and many ships had been lost or damaged in these waters.

Even so, people refused to believe that the *Waratah* could have been lost. Two Royal Navy cruisers began searching on 31 July, but returned ten days later having found nothing. The Australian government chartered a ship to search for a month: the *Severn* steamed for 2,700 miles (4,345 kilometres), but came back empty-handed. The steamer *Sabine* searched for 88 days, from 11 September until 7 December, and covered 14,000 miles (22,500 kilometres), going as far as the fringes of the Antarctic; still there was nothing. On 15 December, the *Waratah* was finally posted missing at Lloyd's.

Soon the rumours and hoaxes began – messages in bottles washed up in Australia; tales of white children raised by African tribes near the coast; men claiming to be survivors, ready to sell their stories to the newspapers; and clairvoyants who could tell where the wreck lay. But the *Waratah* remains one of the most enduring of maritime enigmas and, to this day, her fate has never been ascertained. It is almost certain that she foundered suddenly in bad weather, but whether this was due to poor stability, structural failure or a freak wave will probably never be known.

A Board of Inquiry, held in London in 1910–11, found that the *Waratah* was seaworthy, but was lost suddenly in violent seas that caused her to capsize. The board recommended further studies be carried out on the stability of ocean-going ships.

THE DISAPPEARANCE OF *USS SCORPION*, 1968

Nineteen-sixty-eight was a bad year for submarines – no less than four were lost with all hands in the space of five months, causing the deaths of 327 men. One of these disasters involved the American nuclear submarine USS *Scorpion*, which was heading west across the Atlantic from the Mediterranean to the naval yard at Norfolk, Virginia, when she disappeared. She sent a routine progress signal at 8 am on 21 May, giving her position as 250 miles (402 kilometres) west of the Azores, then nothing more was heard from her.

A major search operation was mounted, and the wreck of the *Scorpion* was finally discovered five months later, when she was photographed lying on the ocean floor at a depth of 10,000 feet (3,000 metres), 460 miles (740 kilometres) south-west of the Azores. But the discovery raised many

Left: A mass grave was dug in the churchyard of St Keverne in Cornwall for the victims of the Mohegan disaster.

Above: *The disappearance of the SS Waratah, seen here in harbour, is one of the most enduring mysteries of the sea.*

questions, among them the reasons for her being so far south of her last reported position and for her hull being intact, as revealed by the photographs. When the *USS Thresher* had been lost in deep water in 1963, along with her crew of 129 – the world's first and worst nuclear submarine loss – her hull had been crushed by the immense pressure and

shattered into thousands of pieces, at a depth of only 8,400 feet (2,560 metres). Surely the *Scorpion* should have been crushed too.

Nothing further was revealed by the authorities, and the *Scorpion's* fate remained a mystery until 1993, when the US Navy issued a report detailing the true findings of its investigation. Apparently, one of the submarine's torpedoes had malfunctioned, and its motor had started while it was still inside the torpedo room. Unable to stop the motor, the captain decided that the best course of action was to jettison the torpedo, so the tube was prepared and the torpedo launched. Unfortunately, the torpedo's guidance system became active and it locked on to the nearest target – the *USS Scorpion*. The torpedo blew a hole in the boat's conning tower, and she sank into the ocean depths, taking 99 crew with her. (The hole equalized the internal and external pressures, so the hull was not crushed.)

THE LOSS OF THE *DERBYSHIRE*, 1980

Sometime on, or about, 9 September 1980, the bulk carrier *Derbyshire* disappeared without trace during a typhoon in the Pacific Ocean, south of Japan. She was 965 feet (294 metres) long with a beam of 144 feet (44 metres) – the size of three football pitches – and had a deadweight tonnage of 169,050 dwt (473,325 cubic metres). She was the biggest British-registered ship ever to be declared a total loss, and the biggest vessel ever posted missing at Lloyd's. And whatever happened to her, she went down so fast that there was no time to send out any distress call at all.

The *Derbyshire* had been built four years previously, being one of six sister ships constructed at Swan Hunter's Haverton Hill yard between 1971 and 1976. On her last voyage, she took on 155,700 tons (158,185 tonnes) of iron ore at the Sept Isles terminal in Quebec, and sailed for Kawasaki, Japan, on 11 July 1980. On board were 42 officers and crew, and the wives of two of the officers. Her last radio messages were received on 9 September, giving her position as 230 miles (370 kilometres) east-south-east of Okinawa, hove to in Tropical Storm Orchid, ETA at Kawasaki 14 September. She was never heard from again.

An air and sea search discovered an oil slick close to the *Derbyshire*'s last reported position, and a sample taken from it proved to be identical to the fuel oil carried on board. The ship was declared a total loss. But what had happened? The *Derbyshire* was double-skinned and well maintained. She was owned in the UK by a reputable line. She was registered in Britain. She was classed with Lloyd's Register. She was crewed by competent British seamen. And she had been lost without trace in a storm that was easily survived by other, smaller ships. But the British Government decided that her loss did not even warrant a formal investigation.

There the matter would have rested had it not been for the stubborn determination of the relatives of the lost seamen, who formed the *MV Derbyshire* Family Association (DFA) to campaign for a public inquiry, and to increase public awareness of the appalling safety record of large bulk carriers – no less than 149 such ships were lost between 1980 and 1994, along with the lives of 1,144 seamen. Their efforts finally shamed the government into holding an official inquiry in 1987, but it merely concluded that the ship 'was probably overcome by the forces of nature'. When asked what recommendations could be made, the inquiry replied, 'As the cause of the loss has not been established . . . this question cannot be answered'.

Little consideration was given to the theory that the ship had suffered major structural failure, a hypothesis put forward by experts representing the DFA and supported by evidence of cracking in the hulls of the *Derbyshire*'s sister ships. An expedition, sponsored by the International Transport Workers Federation, located the wreck of the *Derbyshire* in 1994 and filmed the wreckage, using a remotely operated vehicle (similar to that which filmed the wreck of the *Titanic*). Their findings strongly suggested that the ship had suffered a catastrophic break-up on the surface, and prompted the government to commission a report from Lord Donaldson. He concluded that a further expedition was required, which was mounted in 1996 and 1997. At the time of writing (early 1998), the investigation into the loss of the *Derbyshire* had just been reopened.

Lord Donaldson noted in his 1995 report: 'The members of the *MV Derbyshire* Family Association have played a major role in ensuring that the cause of the loss of the *Derbyshire* is and remains a matter of public concern . . . directly and indirectly their persistence has made a major contribution to the cause of maritime safety.'

CHAPTER TEN

SURVIVAL AND RESCUE

Disasters at sea have claimed countless lives through the centuries, but a fortunate and
resourceful few have managed to survive against the odds. Shipwreck stories have a universal fascination,
being rich in examples of heroism and cowardice, incredible feats of skill and seamanship, and
accounts of inspiring leadership and dogged determination to survive.

Such tales celebrate the eternal daunt-
lessness of the human spirit, and the
innate altruism that compels us to go to the
aid of another human being in distress.

CAPTAIN BLIGH'S VOYAGE IN AN OPEN BOAT, 1789

The mutiny on *HMS Bounty* is one of the most
famous incidents in British maritime history. The
many books and films on the subject have
concentrated on the tensions between Lieutenant
William Bligh and his friend and first mate Fletcher
Christian, the adventures of the mutineers, and their
subsequent court martial. Generally, however, they
make only passing reference to what is widely
regarded as one of the most remarkable feats of
seamanship and survival on record.

When Fletcher Christian wrested control of the
Bounty on 28 April 1789, he put Bligh and the 18
men who remained loyal into the ship's launch and
cast them adrift amid the islands of Tonga. There
were 19 people in an open boat – only 23 feet (7
metres) long and 7 feet (2 metres) wide – with
limited food and water, thousands of miles from the
nearest outpost of European civilization. At that
time, very few ships ventured into the western
Pacific, and no one expected the *Bounty* to return to
Britain for another year at least. They were utterly
alone and without hope of rescue.

Fortunately, Christian had allowed them to take
a compass and sextant, a navigation book, some
food and water, and a mast and sails, although the

mutineers' later actions showed that they assumed
their former shipmates would die. First, Bligh sailed
to the nearby island of Tofoa to obtain more food
and water, but one of the men was killed by the
natives, and the party was forced to flee. On 3 May,
he turned the boat's head to the west, having
decided to make for the Dutch trading settlement on
the Indonesian island of Timor, nearly 4,000 miles
(6,400 kilometres) away.

It is a testament to Bligh's skills in seamanship,
navigation and leadership that he succeeded in
doing this without losing any more of his men. He
dished out rations – often as little as an ounce (28
grams) of biscuit and a gill (0.14 litres) of water a
day, and an occasional teaspoon of rum – with an
iron hand, and guided his boat safely through gales
and reefs for six long weeks, before entering the
harbour at Timor on 14 June. Bligh's accomplish-
ment is that this triumph of seamanship and
navigation still ranks as one of the longest successful voyages ever made in an open boat.

THE WRECK OF THE *FORFARSHIRE*, 1838

The paddle-steamer *Forfarshire* was one of the first
steamships to ply the east coast route between
Scotland and London, and on the night of 6
September 1838, she was struggling northwards
against a gale, bound from Hull to Dundee with 63
people on board. Soon after midnight, her engines
failed while she was off St Abbs Head. The captain
ordered some scraps of sail to be set and ran back
southwards before the wind, planning to shelter in

Above: Grace Darling, daughter of
the Farne Islands lighthouse keeper,
became a national heroine after the
wreck of the Forfarshire in 1838.

Opposite: Captain William
Bligh and his loyal crew were cast
adrift in an open boat after
Fletcher Christian seized control of
HMS Bounty.

Above: *The Antarctic explorer Sir Ernest Shackleton and his men survived unbelievable hardship after their ship, the* Endurance, *was crushed by pack ice the Weddell Sea in 1915.*

Opposite: *The* Endurance *trapped in the ice of Antartica.*

the lee of the Farne Islands. But he misjudged his position, and at 3.45 am, just on the point of dropping anchor, the *Forfarshire* ran on to the notorious Harcar rocks.

The ship broke in two and the after part, with the first-class passengers still inside, sank immediately. One of the boats was lowered, and seven crew and one passenger jumped aboard, but they were swept away before they could pick up any more survivors. A small group of 13 people managed to clamber from the wreckage on to the exposed rocks, where they huddled together for warmth as the gale raged around them. By dawn, four of them had died of exposure, but their plight was noticed by Grace Darling, the 23-year-old daughter of the Longstone Lighthouse keeper, who lived on nearby Brownsman Island.

Grace and her father, William, launched their coble (a heavily built 21-foot/6-metre rowing boat) and pulled through the stormy seas to the Harcar rocks, a distance of almost a mile. They picked up five of the survivors and took them back to their house on Brownsman. Then her father and two of the sailors returned to pick up the others. Grace tended the survivors for three days until the weather allowed them to get ashore, when her exploits were splashed across the pages of the national newspapers, making her one of Britain's first media celebrities. Grace was a reluctant heroine, however, and shied away from the publicity; she died of tuberculosis aged only 26.

THE GREAT ANTARCTIC RESCUE, 1916

Although the British Imperial Trans-Antarctic Expedition, led by Sir Ernest Shackleton, failed in its objective of making the first crossing of the frozen continent from sea to sea, nevertheless it created one of the great legends of polar exploration.

The expedition's ship, *Endurance*, with 28 expedition members, departed the island of South Georgia on 5 December 1914 and headed south into the Weddell Sea, but she soon became stuck in the pack ice. There she remained, drifting slowly with the pack for ten months until, on 21 November 1915, she was crushed by the ice and sank. The men had had plenty of time to unload supplies, along

with three small boats, and they continued their vigil, camped on the ice, for another five months. On 9 April, the ice began to break up, and the expedition took to the boats, sailing to Elephant Island, near the tip of the Antarctic Peninsula.

No one knew where they were, and the rest of the world's attention was caught up in World War 1 – they would have to rely on their initiative and organize their own rescue. To this end, Shackleton and five other men set sail in the *James Caird*, the largest and most seaworthy of the three boats (although only 22 feet, 6 inches/7 metres long), in an attempt to reach the whaling stations of South Georgia, 800 miles away, which they had left almost 18 months previously. They suffered gales, ice and constant soakings for 16 days at sea, and survived a hurricane (which later they learned had claimed a 500-ton/508-tonne steamer with all hands), before landing at King Haakon's Sound on the west coast of South Georgia on 10 May 1916.

From there, Shackleton and two companions climbed over glaciers and mountain ridges for 25 miles (40 kilometres), walking continuously for 36 hours, before reaching a Norwegian whaling station on the east coast. The whalers organized a ship immediately and picked up the three men left on the west coast the next day, but the southern winter was closing in, and it took Shackleton four attempts in four different ships before he successfully battled through the ice to reach the 22 men who had been left behind on Elephant Island. The Chilean steamer *Yelcho* finally rescued them on 30 August 1916, more than nine months after the *Endurance* had sunk, and not a single life had been lost.

Unfortunately, some of the expedition members lost their lives in the war after returning to civilization, one of them a mere six months after being rescued. Shackleton himself died suddenly of a heart attack on 5 January 1922, the day after arriving in South Georgia to begin yet another Antarctic expedition.

THE REMARKABLE JOURNEY OF POON LIM, 1942

The record for the longest survival alone on a raft belongs to a Chinese seaman called Poon Lim. He

Above: Tony Bullimore's yacht, Exide Challenger, *lost its keel and capsized during a storm in the Southern Ocean in 1997.*

Amazon, having drifted for 133 days. Weak, exhausted and close to death, he was taken to hospital in Belem, where he made a full recovery. He told the authorities of the other raft he had seen, but nothing was ever found.

SURVIVAL IN THE SOUTHERN OCEAN, 1997

The most famous survival story of recent years was the rescue of Tony Bullimore and Thierry Dubois from their capsized yachts, 1,400 miles (2,250 kilometres) south of Perth, Western Australia. The two men were competing in the Vendée Globe single-handed, non-stop, round-the-world race when they were caught in a storm in the Southern Ocean. Bullimore's yacht, *Exide Challenger*, lost her keel and capsized in the huge seas kicked up by the storm. All the hatches had been closed, and at first very little water came into the upturned yacht, but within a few hours of the capsize, the thrashing of the main boom stove in a cabin window. Freezing cold water flooded into the inverted hull until only a few feet of airspace remained. Soaked and shivering, Bullimore put on a survival suit and activated his Argos distress beacon.

Although there was little danger of the yacht sinking in the immediate future – she had a foam-sandwich hull with watertight buoyancy compartments – the disaster had occurred in one of the remotest parts of the world, more than 1,000 miles (1,600 kilometres) from the nearest inhabited land. The French authorities picked up the satellite-relayed signals not only from Bullimore's distress beacon, but also from that of a second Vendée Globe competitor, Thierry Dubois in *Pour Amnesty International*, who had suffered a capsize in the same region. They alerted the Maritime Rescue Co-ordination Centre in Canberra, which began the biggest peacetime search-and-rescue operation that Australia had ever seen. Royal Australian Air Force aircraft searched the target area, while the Royal Australian Navy frigate *Adelaide* steamed southwards from Fremantle, three days' sail away from the stricken yachts.

One of the aircraft located the two yachts on Monday afternoon and dropped a liferaft to Dubois,

was a steward on the British cargo ship *Benlomond*, operated by the famous Ben Line, which sailed from Cape Town on 10 November 1942, bound for Paramaribo in Dutch Guiana (now Surinam). On board were 47 officers and men. At around midday on 23 November, when the ship was a few hundred miles off the Brazilian coast, she was torpedoed by an Italian submarine – the torpedo hit the engine room and the *Benlomond* sank within minutes.

Poon Lim managed to swim to a raft that had floated free, then saw another raft nearby with five people on it, but they soon lost sight of each other. There was emergency food and water on his raft, and when that ran out, he lived on what little in the way of fish and seabirds he could catch. Eventually, he was picked up on 5 April 1943 by a Brazilian fisherman off Salinopolis, near the mouths of the

who was lashed to the keel of his upturned yacht, but of Bullimore there was no sign. The planes even tried dropping hydrophones into the sea beside *Exide Challenger* to listen for signs of life, but they heard nothing. Meanwhile, *Adelaide* was getting closer, and on Wednesday the ship's helicopter winched Dubois from the liferaft, but the weather was steadily deteriorating with another gale on the way.

Adelaide reached *Exide Challenger* on Wednesday afternoon and lowered three seamen in an inflatable boat. Within minutes of banging on the upturned hull, the sailors saw Bullimore surface beside the yacht, having dived out through the upturned companionway.

Back on the frigate, the ship's doctor found him in remarkably good condition, suffering only from minor frostbite and missing the tip of a little finger. Four days later, Bullimore and Dubois received a hero's welcome at Fremantle harbour, where 5,000 people lined the dockside. After the rescue, there was criticism of an event that encourages racing yachts to venture into the remote and dangerous waters of the Southern Ocean. The considerable cost of the rescue was borne by the Australian taxpayer, but the government claimed that the incident had provided valuable experience, and that similar amounts would have been spent on training exercises.

CRITICISMS

After the rescue there was criticism of an event that encourages racing yachts to venture into the remote waters of the Southern Ocean.

Left: *Tony Bullimore is comforted by seamen of the Australian navy after being rescued from his capsized yacht.*